The Undersea Discoveries
of Jacques-Yves Cousteau

THE SHARK:
Splendid Savage of the Sea

**The Undersea Discoveries
of Jacques-Yves Cousteau**

THE SHARK:

Splendid Savage of the Sea

Jacques-Yves Cousteau

and Philippe Cousteau

Doubleday & Company, Inc.
Garden City, New York
1970

Translated from the French by Francis Price

Library of Congress Catalog Card Number 69-13004
Copyright © 1970 by Jacques-Yves Cousteau
Printed in the Federal Republic of Germany
First Edition in the United States of America

CONTENTS

INTRODUCTION
Jacques-Yves Cousteau

It has been more than two years since my ship, the *Calypso,* left Monaco to carry out its longest and most fascinating voyage. We have already dived, camera in hand, among the sharks of the Red Sea and the Indian Ocean. We have explored the archipelagoes and the lost isles of the Maldives; the Seychelles, Socotra, Aldabra, the Iles Glorieuses, the Europa Atoll.* We have rediscovered, on the banks of reefs, the prehistoric levels imposed on the sea by the cycle of glacial eras; we have danced with marine creatures who resembled the guests at a masked ball; we have clung to the fins of toothed whales and baleen whales and, for some of them, we have annotated the journal of their travels. We have uncovered marine fossils in the mountains of Malagasy; we have domesticated Pepito and Cristobal, two sea lions from the Cape of Good Hope, explored the wrecks of the island of St. Helena, sought the treasures of the Silver Bank shoal in the Bahamas, dived in our "saucer" to the bottom of Lake Titicaca, lived with the sea elephants of Guadalupe Island. And now we are preparing to cross the Pacific, diving and filming in the Galapagos and Society islands, at Noumea, on the Great Barrier Reef, and in the Sunda Islands between the Indian Ocean and the Pacific. I am translating this long and marvelous voyage into a vast and colorful cinematographic fresco, destined for the television screens of the

*The Maldive Islands, in the Indian Ocean, run north and south off the southwest coast of India. The Seychelles are in the Somali Basin, north-northeast of Madagascar (the Malagasy Republic), which is the great island lying off the east coast of Africa. Socotra is off the Gulf of Aden and the easternmost point of Africa. Aldabra is north of the Comoro Islands, which are to the west of Madagascar's northern tip. The Iles Glorieuses are northeast of the Comoro Islands. The Europa Atoll lies in the Mozambique Channel, between Africa's Mozambique coast and Madagascar.

entire world. I have put into it all the experience I have acquired in the course of thirty-three years of diving, all my love for nature and for the sea.

What is not apparent on the screen is the almost insurmountable difficulty of such an enterprise: the years of technical preparation, of research and documentation; the financial obstacles involving substantial personal sacrifices for a crew of one hundred and fifty men; the thousands of dives in conventional diving suits, the hundreds of dives in the saucer, the hours passed shivering in the cold water or in the decompression chamber, the nights spent repairing a piece of essential equipment or a flooded camera, the tempests of sand, the tropical cyclones, the accidents that occur in a ship in the middle of an ocean, the agonies we experience when we lose trace of a diver or a saucer — and lastly the most direct of all these risks, those of which Philippe is writing here — those which always accompany any meeting with sharks.

The Undersea Discoveries
of Jacques-Yves Cousteau

THE SHARK:
Splendid Savage of the Sea

ONE:

First Encounter

A meeting with a great blue shark. The story behind making the film on the behavior of sharks. Description of the *Calypso* and the team.

Philippe Cousteau's narrative

His entire form is fluid, weaving from side to side; his head moves slowly from left to right, right to left, timed to the rhythm of his motion through the water. Only the eye is fixed, focused on me, circling within the orbit of the head, in order not to lose sight for a fraction of a second of his prey or, perhaps, of his enemy.

His skin is creased with a thousand silky furrows at every movement of his body, emphasizing each pattern of incredible muscle. The crystalline water has ceased to exist; he is there in the unbelievable purity of the void and nothing separates us any longer.

There is no threat, no movement of aggression. Only a sort of nonchalant suspicion is apparent in the movements and attitudes of the shark, and yet he generates fear. Amazed and startled, filled with apprehension, circling with movements as slow and silent as possible, I try to keep him constantly in front of me.

There is something of the miraculous in the suddenness of his appearance as well as in his infinite grace; the surface of the water is far above and its absence contributes to the magical quality of the moment. He turns once more, and the sphere he encompasses expands or contracts, in accordance with his own primitive impulses or the subtle changes of the current. His silent

The most beautiful shark of all. This is a blue shark demonstrating one of his sinuous swimming movements. He is accompanied by three pilot fish. One of them is near the gills on the right side of his head. The blue shark appears out of nowhere in the middle of the ocean. He is definitely one of the dangerous sharks, one of the solitary species never running in packs.

circling is a ballet governed by untraceable mechanisms. The blue tranquillity of his form surrounds me with the sensation of a web of murderous and yet beautiful force. I have the feeling that I have accompanied his circular voyage since the beginning of time. His configuration is perfect. Suddenly, the idea that he deserves killing comes to me like a shock and instantly shatters the spell. Murder is the real function of this ideal form, of this icy-blue camouflage, and of that enormous, powerful tail. The water has returned to my consciousness, I can feel it again, gentle and flowing between my fingers, solid against my palms. I am one hundred and ten feet below the surface, in the clear, deep water of the Indian Ocean. With thirty minutes of air remaining and a camera in my hand, I am far from being an easy prey. Our circling has, in fact, gone

This is a side view of the blue shark under different lighting. You can see his wide black eye, his constantly open mouth engulfing the water that goes out through the gills. Underneath his mouth, attached by an overhead suction device, you can see a remora fish—the shark's traveling companion—eating the crumbs, leftovers from the shark's meals. The blue shark is by far the most majestic of all sharks. You can see the shape of his muscles in the back of his head and on the sides. The underside of his belly is snow white. You don't see his teeth now because they are retracted, lying flat on the inside of his mouth or palate.

on for only a few seconds and already I can hear the irregular snorting of the engine in the surveillance craft above me.

The great blue shark continues his approach toward me in the unchanging manner which has been that of his race throughout its existence. He is really a superb animal, almost seven feet in length, and I know, since I have often seen them before, that his jaw is lined with seven rows of teeth, as finely honed as the sharpest razor. I have already begun to ascend slowly toward the surface, simulating a few movements of attack whenever his orbit brings him sufficiently close. He perceives the slightest pressure wave from my smallest movement, analyzes every change in acidity or in the vaguest of odors, and he will never allow himself to be surprised by an abrupt movement. He can swim at a speed of more than thirty knots and his attack would probably be impossible to parry. But he is still circling slowly around me, making use of the cautiousness that has protected his species since its first appearance on this planet more than one hundred million years ago. I know that the circles are growing inexorably smaller and that I will probably succeed in repelling his first attack, but I also know that this will not discourage him. Startled for a moment, he will resume the circle of hunger, his attacks will become more and more frequent, and in the end he will break through my feeble defense and his jaws will close on the first bite of my flesh. Drawn by invisible signals, other sharks of the open sea will appear, climbing from the lowest depths or slicing the surface with the knife of their dorsal fins. And then it will be the scramble for the spoils, a frenzy of hunger, of bloody and irresistible strength and horror. For this is the way of the great sharks of the open sea.

I climb back into our surveillance boat, the *Zodiac,* after a last glance at that flawless silhouette and the great staring eye, already regretting the impression of unconquerable power and exalting confrontation, cursing my weakness and being grateful for my fear. I look at the others, companions in dives like this one; burned by the sun, wrinkled by the sea, they look at me and understand: there is a shark beneath us.

Stretched out on the burning rubber of the *Zodiac's* seats, already numbed by the heat and the sun, I think back to all the events that have brought us here to the middle of the Indian Ocean. It is an effort — an enjoyable effort — to recall the beginnings of our adventure.

In the spring of 1966 I was in Hollywood, completing work on a film on the subject of the Precontinent III experiment. I had made this film for the National Geographic Society in Washington, during the thirty days that I and five other divers had spent in our "home" on a ledge three hundred feet below the surface of the Mediterranean. It was a fifty-eight-minute color documentary, expressly produced for television use. As it happened, the company that produces films for the National Geographic Society is Wolper Productions, Inc., whose home offices are on Sunset Boulevard in Los Angeles. It was because of this that my father and I made the acquaintance of the man whose faith and enthusiasm would later permit us to set out on a series of unforgettable adventures: David Wolper. For a long time past, my father had been thinking of a series of films on the sea, designed for television, but the project had come up against the ingrained habits of Madison Avenue and had never been realized. Then, suddenly, David Wolper suggested that we make twelve films of one hour each on subjects of our own choice, and with financial backing sufficient to assure us of more than adequate equipment. Obviously, it was going to be necessary to secure even more financial support, but, having completed three or four films as a result of the agreement reached with David, we were confident that we could fill out our budget from the funds obtained through release of these films in other parts of the world.

The discussions on the terms of our contract took place in New York, and I remember the many evenings spent in conference with lawyers and technicians, dragging on far into the night, and followed by lengthy discussions between my father and myself in our hotel room, as we elaborated on the fantastic projects we had in mind. There was nothing to stop us now: we were going to visit all the seas of the world, equipped with completely new and up-to-date matériel; we would find and film the coelacanth in his hidden depths, dive with the giant calamary squid of the Humboldt Current, and rediscover the galleons of Christopher Columbus. Thanks to David's enthusiasm, and then to his successor, Bud Rifkin's, we would be able to do everything that fascinated us, and above all we would be able to do it with a camera, to fix on film everything we loved and found marvelous in the sea.

The first film of the series was scheduled to be the one most likely to intrigue and attract the attention of viewers, and what maritime subject is more fascinating to everyone than the shark? It is a legendary animal, known to all, even to those who live far from the sea.

It was for this reason that we were now aboard the *Zodiac*, on our way back to the *Calypso* after this magnificent dive. The *Calypso*, a 130-foot converted minesweeper, was the ship on which we had carried out many past experiments, but until this time our work had been of a far more scientific nature. Hydrology, biology, geology — all the sciences of the sea, and all kinds of serious, dedicated scientists had been the *raison d'être* of the *Calypso*. Now, for her cinematographic mission, she had been entirely modified and refitted. The scientific winches and scoops had made way for one-man submarines, and the research laboratories had become photographic darkrooms. (A sketch of the *Calypso* on page 246 shows how she was organized and fitted.)

Each of the two 500-horsepower engines had been completely reconditioned before we set out, in preparation for a voyage that would last for five years. The crew's quarters in the forward section of the hull had been arranged to provide space for six more men — film technicians or additional divers. In

The *Calypso* sailing the Indian Ocean, mounting the swells that forewarn of the coming monsoon.

Captain Bougaran, skipper of the *Calypso* during the greater part of the shark trip.

Albert Falco, one of the older members of the crew. A renowned diver, Falco has been Jacques-Yves Cousteau's companion for many years and his right arm on many projects. He is the pilot of all our deep-sea vehicles, and has brought much valuable knowledge back from his numerous trips underwater.

Jean-Paul Bassaget. He was the first lieutenant on the shark expedition, and is now the skipper of the *Calypso*. He is tough, always ready and willing.

The moments before a dive are always exciting. We never know what we are up against or what we are about to discover. Philippe Cousteau is standing in the center, and Canoë Kientzy is sitting to the right. Bernard Delemotte has his back to the camera. We are aboard one of our launches in very flat, calm water. One of the islands is visible in the far background. Hazy days such as this are unusual.

Bernard Mestre. He is our intellectual sailor. He holds a bachelor's degree in literature, yet he is a simple sailor on board the *Calypso,* having spent most of his life on board ships. He enjoys working on deck, as well as diving, and he usually keeps the ship's logbook.

the aft hold there were two one-man submarines, capable of reaching depths of more than 1500 feet, while just above them, on the rear deck, a hydraulic crane was installed to lift them from the hold and set them in the water, without manual effort and without fear of the swell of the sea. On the main deck, the "diving center," which also served as a working post for the electricians, was filled with entirely new diving equipment. The wardroom, the kitchen, and all the other interiors had been refitted.

On the upper deck, a new stateroom had been added to the captain's bridge, and a television control room had been fitted out next to the radio shack. A new radar, larger windows, and two chest-high map tables had completely altered the aspect of the bridge itself. Everywhere, including the observation chamber set beneath the prow, closed-circuit television cameras kept the bridge abreast of whatever was happening, either on board ship or beneath the surface of the water ahead of the hull. All in all, the ship was a tool perfectly adapted to its mission. Her fast small boats could carry a camera man to the locale of any event at any time. In the hold, there was a hot-air balloon that would make it possible for me to film all the operations from above, or even to discover some things that might escape a lookout on the deck. In addition to the indispensable smaller equipment — lenses and several light cameras — the equipment for filming included two 35-millimeter and two 16-millimeter Arriflex cameras, two 16-millimeter Eclair cameras, and three quartz-synchronized Perfectone sound recorders, which permit the camera and the recorder to be separated.

The undersea equipment included twelve cameras manufactured in our own workshops in Marseilles. Of these, four were for filming in 35-millimeter and the rest for 16-millimeter. For lighting, in both the open air and the water, we used quartz lamps of either 1000, 750, or 250 watts, in autonomous battery-powered units or powered by a 110-volt source on board the *Calypso*.

Our diving gear was now completely streamlined by a plastic shell that

Michel Deloire, a close friend of Philippe Cousteau's for many years. Deloire was a stand-by oceanaut on the Conshelf Three experiment in 1965, to replace Philippe if anything happened to him before down date. He is an extremely skilled and talented cameraman-photographer. Deloire was with us from the beginning of this expedition, and shot some of the most beautiful footage ever taken in the water. Also he is an excellent diver, and most of his work takes place under the sea. We also have topside cameramen, like Jacques Renoir, but Michel is our chief cameraman and often handles the camera topside too.

This is Canoë Kientzy. His real name is Raymond Kientzy, but we've always known him as Canoë. He is one of our chief divers on the *Calypso*. He was with us during a good part of the shark trip. His enthusiasm and perfect knowledge of the sea made our expedition easier and more successful.

Marcel Soudre. Fascinated with fishing and trolling, he was one of our divers during the shark expedition.

Bernard Delemotte, also an old friend of Philippe Cousteau's, and a diver on the *Calypso* for many years. He is now ranked as chief diver, supervising the diving crew and all the equipment. His insight into the behavior of the animals of the sea is remarkable.

Paul Zuéna. He was first mate on board the *Calypso* during the trip. He knows the business of running a ship and keeping it fit, inside and out. He keeps the equipment in top shape, and seamanship holds no mystery for him. He would be worthy of a much larger ship—something like the four- or five-masted Cape Horn-type clipper of former days.

Serge Foulon is a young diver who was with us for a time but left. Very much at ease in the water, Serge is a witty fellow, always graceful in the water during filming. He also served as our cook during land expeditions.

Bernard Chauvellin. Bernard was second lieutenant on the shark expedition, and is now the first lieutenant on board.

enclosed not only the four bottles of air compressed into tanks of specially welded steel, but also an ultrasonic telephone for communication with the other divers. A radio for use on the surface and the batteries for our lamps were mounted on the helmet. This helmet, which was also made of plastic, contained receivers for the two communications systems and a highly directional quartz tube governed by a switch placed to one side. A single-piece insulating coverall completed the diving suit. Thus equipped, a diver gains almost 30 per cent in freedom of movement and swims more rapidly with less effort. Designed and manufactured by the engineers of the Centre d'Etudes Marines Avancées (CEMA) in Marseilles, this equipment was the realization of my father's old dream of increasing the efficiency of, and adding an overall completeness to, traditional diving gear. And despite the lack of enthusiasm of our "old" divers, too-long accustomed to their traditional equipment, the new autonomous units represented the first notable progress in the matter of self-contained diving equipment since the invention of the Cousteau-Gagnan aqualung.

In October 1966, we were ready to get underway on a voyage to check out both our new matériel and our techniques. For this, we had decided to use a smaller ship, the *Espadon,* a converted trawler equipped with prototypes of all the equipment to be used on the *Calypso.* We also planned to test our 16-millimeter cameras and two completely new types of film, Ektachrome 7241 and 7242, which had just been put on the market by the Eastman Kodak Company. The expedition was to last three months. It was made up of ten men under the command of Albert Falco, and had as its goal a study of the sharks of the Red Sea.

In February 1967, enriched by the experience acquired on the *Espadon* and having modified our equipment to eliminate its defects, we embarked on the *Calypso.* As we left the port of Monaco, crowds on the wharves showered us with flowers and confetti. The Prince of Monaco and Princess Grace had made a point of paying a personal visit to the ship and, as testimony of their good wishes, had left with us a magnificent St. Hubert dog,* whom we christened Zoom.

---

*The St. Hubert race was bred by the monks of St. Hubert in France in the middle ages. Because of their qualities as hunting dogs and of their power as well as their gentleness, the ownership of such dogs soon became the sole privilege of the kings of France and of the monks of St. Hubert. From the St. Hubert dog a more popular breed was created and became more successful, i.e., the bloodhound.

Any departure on a sea voyage is a glorious moment, but that one was the most splendid of all. A kind of miracle had just taken place. In the age of efficiency, of the scientific imperative, and the law of profitable return, we were leaving with no precise goals, no Draconian demands on our time, no accounts to render to anyone, free to journey wherever our fancy led us. Our only task, our profession, was to see. In a time of superspecialization, we became the farseeing eyes of all those who could not or would not journey themselves. We were akin to those knights-errant who traveled across the world and returned to tell the king the news of the Holy Land or of Mauretania. We were different in the sense that we would bring the story of our adventures not to a solitary king, but to millions of people. When one thinks of it, however, the task becomes enormous. We could imagine each of our future viewers, and know he would be hoping that we brought back accounts of things that were beautiful, true, and intellectually rewarding. Each of them was investing some degree of confidence in us, and this implied a heavy responsibility. We could no more deceive this confidence, this patience, this need for information on the marvels of the deep than we could have abandoned a blind man we might have been guiding across a busy street. Although we had no timetable to respect, no itinerary to follow, we nonetheless had a mission, and we were determined to carry out this mission to the fullest extent of our strength and our enthusiasm.

In a very short time we were out of sight of the rock of Monaco and of the Museum of the Sea which crowns it. Everyone on board shared in my joy and excitement. They were all companions of many years' standing — some had been with my father since 1951; all of them knew their work to perfection and the majority were capable of successfully carrying out three or four different functions. The captain of the *Calypso,* Roger Maritano, had occupied this post for several years, as had Captain Bougaran, who succeeded him. Their first and second lieutenants — Jean-Paul Bassaget and Bernard Chauvellin respectively — were young and competent, in addition to being excellent divers. In charge of our engines was the oldest member of the crew, René Robino, who had been with us ever since our first voyage. With implacable energy and precision, Maurice Léandri directed the team that kept the ship seaworthy. Our two chief divers were Raymond Kientzy and Albert Falco, whom we had nicknamed Canoë and Bébert. They had both joined the *Calypso* at the exciting time of our salvage of the wreck of a Greek galley just outside the harbor of Marseilles. I shared the underwater camerawork with my friends

Jean Morgan, the cook. He can make fish taste like rabbit, and he can vary a menu of tuna about twenty-five ways. He is worthy of the best restaurants, and makes life on board a constant state of euphoria with his distinctive cooking. Morgan is a native of Brittany.

Jean-Marie France, one of our mechanics. A soft-spoken, discreet, gentle person, he has never been heard to say anything that was unnecessary. France can fix anything from an outboard motor to one of the main engines of the *Calypso* in less time than it takes a team of ten other mechanics.

Raymond Amaddio, the *Calypso's* maître d'hôtel. Interested in everything that goes on aboard ship, besides his own work, Raymond directs his efforts toward keeping the spirit of the crew at its highest level. He gives constant attention to the needs and requests of the crew.

Jacques Renoir, topside cameraman and sometime diver. He is one of the most talented topside photographers to have set foot on board the *Calypso*. His excellent photography made the film very attractive, and recorded all the team's topside actions faithfully.

Philippe Cousteau, September 1967.

Eugène Lagorio. He is the sound engineer for films. Responsible for the synchronized sound sequences of most specials, Eugène also records the sounds of underwater animals. In addition, he is the radio technician on board and handles all electronic-maintenance problems. He is an extremely talented electronician, and his duties also encompass the care of the radar and the operation of all deep-echo-sounding equipment. Eugène is a bright and humorous fellow, a very good companion.

Michel Deloire and Yves Omer, and the on-board tasks with Jacques Renoir. From Eugène Lagorio, our radioman and sound engineer (nicknamed Gégène), to Jean Morgan, our cook, every man on board knew and respected his shipmates. It was a totally solid crew, marked by perfect professional excellence. Frédéric Dumas, who had assisted my father from the very beginning, has become a world authority on undersea archeology, and he is still the counselor whose vast experience of the sea and the creatures that live in it greatly enhanced our chances of success.

In 1951, when I was only ten years old, we had explored the Red Sea with Dumas and Robino. I had dived in the undersea forests of Alboran with Kientzy, and descended into the submerged craters of the Azores with Falco. Fifteen years later, Deloire was my assistant and would be eventually, in case of accident, my replacement in the thirty days of the Precontinent III experiment in survival at three hundred feet beneath the surface. With us also were

René Haon is a sailor aboard the *Calypso,* and was second to Paul Zuéna. He has since been promoted to first mate.

Jean Servelo is our electrician. He is constantly busy with the underwater-lighting equipment and with the ship's own electrical circuits.

Omer and four others, among them André Laban, who directed the work of the little group of oceanauts. We had all, at one time or another, needed or helped the others; we had all confronted the same problems or experienced the same emotions. It was a unified team, formed by my father and molded by his spirit of adventure and his respect for life.

Now, the night of our departure, I joined my father on the captain's bridge and we stood there for a long time, contemplating our world and rediscovering the movement of a ship, which our bodies had forgotten during the months of preparation in Paris and New York. My head was filled with thoughts of that fabulous animal, the redoubtable man-eater, and of the metallic beauty and invincible strength of that incomprehensible monster — the shark.

In six days, we would be at work in the Red Sea, and then the adventure would really have begun.

Roger Chopian is a mechanic, and he can work with machine tools like a musician with his favorite instrument. He can engineer and tool for us the most delicate part of a camera or tape recorder, or the radar, or any engine part that must be replaced. He remains cool under all circumstances.

Joseph François. Doctor François was the medical doctor on the shark trip. His practice has taken him all over the world. He is a fine physician, with an understanding for people and an ability to put them at their ease that makes it pleasanter for his patients to follow his advice or take his medicine. Doctor François was quite successful, during this trip, with all the illnesses that usually plague a ship under tropical conditions. His contribution to the good cheer on board was substantial.

José Ruiz, one of the divers. José made his debut with the *Calypso* team and remained with it. He had his first experience with sharks on this expedition.

Roger Dufrêche, our chief mechanic. Mechanical objects hold no secrets from him, and he can build anything aboard ship that may be requested —from a hot-air-balloon inflater to a new spear for tagging guns.

TWO:
Why Tell of Sharks?
Past experiences.
Encounter in the open sea
with the great *longimanus*.
Threats to modern divers.

Philippe Cousteau's narrative continues

One afternoon in the summer of 1945, on the rocks of a little cove between Sanary and Bandol on the Mediterranean coast of France, my father adjusted two miniature self-contained underwater-breathing units on the shoulders of my brother, Jean-Michel, and myself. Then, holding each of us by the hand, he led us out into a few feet of water at the edge of the rocks. My brother was six and a half years old at the time, and I was four. I remember nothing of this first dive, but I have often been told about it. In our astonishment at the underwater world, we both described aloud everything we saw, with the result that we swallowed quantities of salt water.

Since that day, no creatures of the sea that I have chanced upon have inspired irrational fear in me: none, that is, except the shark. I have, however, been stung or bitten by a certain number of them — moray eels, jellyfish, and even by the lowly sea urchin. I have encountered other species of foreboding aspect, such as sting rays and Manta rays, sea elephants, and both the grampus or killer whale and the sperm whale. But each bite or sting was caused by my own clumsiness in regard to these animals, and not to any malignant aggressiveness on their part. The same thing is true of the shark, which I also do not regard as being a killer without a cause, but I cannot prevent myself from thinking that he is the only animal in the sea who possesses the strength, the tools, and the motivation necessary to inflict on me an irreparable mutilation or even death. He is not, of course, the only animal capable of killing a man; the list of those is a long one. I could cite some few of the most widely known, but such an enumeration would be in no sense exhaustive. Only a biologist could draw up such a list, and a volume titled *Dangerous and Venomous Animals of the Sea* does seem to cover the subject exhaustively, at least as of the present state of our scientific knowledge. In the Persian Gulf and in the waters around Indonesia there exist sea serpents of from one and a half to three feet in length whose venom is fatal, but they avoid man whenever they can. The bite of certain small octopuses of Australia or the burns caused by the tentacles of the Physalia jellyfish can be fatal. A sperm whale or a killer whale can cut a man in two, and the other cetaceans are perfectly capable of breaking the spinal column with a blow of their tail. Even a peaceful dolphin could kill a swimmer, in the same manner in which he disposes of sharks. There also exist sea crocodiles, which haunt the coasts of Indonesia and are greatly feared by the local populations. But none of these animals constitutes a real menace to divers. The majority live either far out at sea or in the greath depths — as, for instance, is the case of the giant squid of the Humboldt Current.

Sharks, however, are everywhere in tropical or temperate waters, and some species, such as the Greenland shark, even live in glacial oceans. They are found at great depths as well as on the surface and even in the estuaries of rivers and in some fresh-water lakes in Latin America. It is, therefore, possible to encounter a shark wherever man ventures on or under the sea, and the encounter can be fatal.

Man has succeeded in eliminating from the surface of the earth the majority of animals and a large number of the insects that could imperil his life. When the race has not been entirely destroyed, what remains of it is generally herded into a reserve, as is the case with the great wild beasts of Africa and India. But in many cases, intensive hunting has so reduced the species as to render any threat from it practically nonexistent.

I do not wish to philosophize on human attitudes, and I can only express my sorrow at the often unjustified destruction of so much richness and beauty. I am ashamed of the out-and-out hypocrisy of some measures, supposedly for the protection of the species, which amount to nothing more than the sale of so many pounds of lion or elephant — at an exorbitant price per pound — to a privileged and wealthy few who would be more at home in a psychiatric clinic than in their "sporting clubs." And I cannot help but express the poignant sense of regret experienced by both my father and myself when we are

Jacques-Yves Cousteau (right) and Philippe Cousteau on the rear deck of the *Calypso,* discussing the order of the day. The background is supplied by a hydraulic crane and one of our one-man submarines.

forced to stand by helplessly and watch the destruction of cetaceans such as the great blue whale, the largest living creature of all time and one that will soon be no more than a memory.

The shark need have no fear of such a fate. The majority of the races of squali, to which sharks belong, are perfectly adapted to their mode of life and their enormous number makes their extermination extremely difficult, if not impossible. This, in turn, makes the shark one of the last of the animals dangerous to man and still uncontrolled. There are squali practically everywhere; almost all of them can be dangerous or deadly, and there still exists no effective form of protection that is easily transportable by one man. This, added to the fact that civilization is at last turning back toward the sea and thereby considerably augmenting the possibility of encounters between man and shark, has lent urgency to the need for a more complete knowledge of shark habits. Several nations have already established laboratories devoted entirely to this task.

There is a mystery attached to the relations between man and shark, and the stranger attitude is perhaps not that of the animal. For a very long period, man was ignorant of the existence of sharks, and until the middle of the sixteenth century there was not even an English word to designate this species: the Spanish word *tiburon* was currently used. To fill out this linguistic note, it might be remarked that the French word for shark — *requin* — stems from "Requiem," the Mass for the dead; reflecting sailors' fear of the appearance of this beast in the waters around them. Some even feared that sighting a shark presaged the death of a member of the crew. In antiquity, there is mention of sharks only in the writings of Herodotus, Aristotle, and Pliny. Pliny, in particular, went so far as to distinguish among four different species of sharks. Before these Greek writers, no precise mention of sharks is to be found, and yet it may be that the first legend relating to the squalus is in the Bible. Linnaeus, the eminent eighteenth-century Swedish naturalist, was convinced that the monster that swallowed Jonah was a great white shark and not a whale. And ever since the Bible many, many other stories have been told of this fantastic animal — most of them horrible. These stories, true or false, have contributed toward creating a psychosis of the shark in all the sailors of the world and even in men who are simply interested in the sea, without the slightest intention of even going near it.

Second in violence only to the monstrous fury of hungry sharks is the blind hatred of man for this species. I have watched and filmed scenes of carnage of implacable cruelty, in which normally quiet and reasonable men used axes to hack at the bodies of sharks they had caught, and then plunged their hands and arms into the blood streaming from the entrails, to extract their hooks and their bait. Floundering about among the gutted carcasses for hours on end, pushing hook and bait back and up to within inches of the quivering jaws they would normally never have gone near, these men were gratifying some obscure form of vengeance.

This psychological factor, this almost automatic loss of self-control on the part of the most hardened man when he finds himself confronted with a shark, is probably responsible for many cases of fatal attack.

Whether it be through the study of human reactions or through a study of the habits of the squalus, our civilization now must establish an effective method of protection against sharks. Unless we do this, our invasion of the oceans will be delayed or made difficult of accomplishment, because the great mass of nonprofessional divers will be afraid and will hesitate to venture into the sea.

Moreover, the shark presents us, on a scientific level, with a very particular case. It has been estimated from the study of fossils that the first sharks made their appearance in the oceans around the beginning of the Cretaceous period of the Mesozoic epoch — approximately a hundred and forty million

Two divers equipped with their new gear—streamlined backpacks, and helmets with individual lights. They are examining a white Gorgonia. Gorgonias are colonies of very tiny animals eating the plankton of the water, and they look like the white hair of an undersea beast.

years ago. And since their first appearance the squali have undergone only insignificant changes. They have survived changes in temperature, in salinity and in types of nourishment, as well as in the level of the waters. They are a living contradiction in the sense that their cartilaginous skeleton is relatively primitive while their reproductive system is complex and developed beyond that of other fish.

Sharks belong to the elasmobranch, or cartilaginous, class of fish, as opposed to the various classes of bony fish. The elasmobranch, in turn, are divided into two subclasses, the holocephalian and the selachian; and it is to this latter subclass that sharks belong. Other cartilaginous fish belonging to this same classification include the small sharks known as dogfish and various species of rays, including the numbfish and the guitar fish.

Jacques-Yves Cousteau's narrative

The reactions of a man confronted by a shark are of an impassioned nature. They are rooted in legend and influenced by tales deserving no credence whatever. The search for objectivity is a discouraging enterprise. I have met several men who have been bitten by sharks and survived serious wounds; their scars had a sinister appearance, particularly to me, since, as a diver, I inevitably identified myself with the victim. Each time this has happened, dozens of questions have flashed through my mind and I have listened avidly to the answers, as if they would at last reveal the truth to me. But this has never eventuated. The majority of the victims were unable to describe what had actually taken place, and others had more or less consciously elaborated their stories. So today, I am reduced to taking into consideration only my own memories, knowing very well that the same mechanism that caused my own reaction to such stories will undoubtedly provoke skepticism on the part of other divers.

With or without special means of protection, alone or in groups, in warm waters as well as cold, it is now thirty-three years that I have been diving, and often in the company of sharks: all kinds of sharks, sharks of every disposition, sharks reputed to be harmless, and sharks known to be deadly. I and my diving companions fear them, laugh at them, admire them, but are forced to resign ourselves to sharing the waters with them. The latent menace

The incredibly blue color of the blue shark's back explains his name. One can see the elegant silhouette of this animal, with his long pectoral fins and his very thin fins on back and underside. He has a keenly pointed snout. He is one of the fastest sharks in the sea. He has remora suckerfish on the right side of his dorsal fin; on the other side swims a pilot fish close by. The unusual size of his pectoral fins gives him great agility in the water. His gills are flared, for he is moving rapidly at this moment, and the water is rushing through them at high speed.

they embody has always been our diving companion, and they have some-times — rarely — chased us from the sea.

But after an experience of three decades, might it not now be time to sum up, to shift through all these personal memories and allot to emotions and indisputable facts their proper places?

In the Mediterranean, sharks are rare and cause few accidents. But their very rarity confers a peculiar solemnity on each encounter. My "first" sharks, at Djerba, were Mediterranean and impressed me unduly, because I had not expected to see them. On the other hand, in the Red Sea, where it is practically impossible to dive among the reefs of the open sea without being surrounded by sharks, coexistence was inevitable and my companions and I very soon became imprudent, almost unaware of their presence. I even sensed in our team the beginnings of a certain affectation of disdain for these inoffensive prowlers, a tendency to feign ignorance of them, to speak of them only in jest. I argued against this form of snobbishness because it could become dangerous, but I was vulnerable to it myself. It is intoxicating for an awkward and vulnerable creature, such as a diver becomes the instant he drops beneath the surface of the water, to imagine himself stronger than a creature far better armed than he. It was in this climate of excessive vanity and confidence in the early years that I dived myself and allowed others to dive, without protection,

This hammerhead shark is one of the rare forms seen on the Red Sea venture. Although its mouth is relatively small compared to its body size, the shark is considered dangerous. It is an awkward creature, and the sight of it generates fear. The strange shape of the head is one of the mysteries of the shark world. Some scientists suggest that it gives better vision, although that has not been proved with any certainty. Others suggest that because the nostrils are separated and located at each end of the hammer-shaped head, the shark has a better directional sense of smell. Hammerhead sharks often congregate and hunt in packs.

in the most dangerous waters. On the reef of João Valente, in the Cape Verde Islands, we jostled or pulled on the tails of animals over twelve feet in length, incomparably more powerful and competent than we awkward intruders with steel bottles on our backs, our field of vision limited by the masks we wore, and caricatures of fins on our feet. The day at João Valente when Dumas and I glimpsed in the distance the pale silhouette of a great white shark (the species that all specialists qualify as a man-eater), we were frozen with terror and instinctively drew closer together. We had seen him before he saw us. But as soon as he became aware of our presence, it was he who was seized with panic; emptying out his intestines, he disappeared with a single flick of his tail. Later, in the Indian Ocean, the same incident occurred on two separate occasions. And each time, the violent emotion brought on in us by the appearance of the great white shark gave way to an unjustified sensation of triumph when he fled at the mere sight of us. Each of these unusual encounters provoked great excitement among us, and with it an excessive confidence in ourselves and a consequent relaxation of security measures.

Deep-sea diving with self-contained breathing equipment brings with it a kind of narcosis, which we christened "intoxication of the depths": it becomes evident anywhere around a depth of a hundred and thirty feet and becomes annoying and even dangerous at depths below two hundred feet. The "intoxication" manifests itself in a sort of euphoria, then in a quickening of some of the senses — the hearing in particular. The sense of reality is reduced, and consequently the instinct of self-preservation. All these symptoms disappear, as if by magic, during the period of return to the surface. It is therefore logical that the depth to which one dives, since it can bring about such psychic upheavals, can also influence the reactions of a diver confronted with sharks. Once, in mid-Atlantic, on board the *Elie Monnier,* we encountered large schools of dolphins, so we brought the ship to a halt while we dived among them, as far down as a hundred to a hundred and fifty feet. The dolphins disappeared within a matter of minutes, but we could still see schools of yellowfinned tuna and great ocean sharks, a hundred or so feet below us. I can remember now the eerie sensations of these insane dives. At about one hundred and fifty feet the surface had practically disappeared and the area of water surrounding me was strangely somber, a blue that was almost black; the intoxication of the depths was there, flooding my entire being, but it seemed to me to be controllable, like the first puff of opium. Mad with liberty, weightless, and completely removed from the world, listening to the beating of my heart in this pelagic silence, I was ready to commit any kind of imprudence. And today I realize that I committed all of them.

Far from the surface, where the sun perhaps was shining, but still more than two miles from the bottom of the sea, lost in water which was black as ink and yet incredibly transparent, because light passed through it without interference, I lost all notion of horizontal and vertical. I could no longer distinguish between up and down. I had only one reference with which to orient myself: the bubbles of air escaping from the pressure tanks on my back. What I felt in the course of these giddy dives was perhaps stranger, even more disconcerting than the impressions felt by the first "space walkers." The astronauts, leaving their capsule, can clearly see the familiar stars and planets, while I felt myself lost in immensity, with no landmarks to guide me. The only reassuring existence in my realm was a somewhat remote one; the boat which I knew — or thought — to be above me, carefully following the traces left on the surface by my air bubbles. It was in this extraordinary atmosphere that sharks made their most dramatic appearance. I still knew little of these sharks of the high seas and I was fascinated by their majesty. They were generally much larger than those of the reefs. There were species of them, at that time, which I was unable to identify. The majority had sharper noses and more clearly defined silhouettes than, for example, the tiger shark. They seemed to be following the schools of dolphins, but maintaining a certain distance from them. When they appeared out of nowhere they made no effort to approach me, but instead changed their course when they were about fifty feet away, as if to keep me in sight. The first time I found myself in this situation, the sighting of the first shark was a violent emotional shock. Framed in light in the darkness of the water, he stood out clearly, in an unreal, terrifying manner. And, certainly as a result of the intoxication caused by the one-hundred-fifty-foot depth at which I was swimming, the admiration and fear I experienced were abruptly transformed into an unreasoning sense of exultation. I swam straight toward the great shark, armed only with my camera, but he drew away from me, keeping the same distance between us. I went on swimming through the blue-black depths, pursuing a silhouette which finally disappeared, diving far down below me; I was alone now, breathing hard, lost, my temples throbbing, my mind disturbed, realizing confusedly that my conduct had been idiotic, but proud of thinking myself capable of putting such a formidable creature to flight. In an element which was not naturally mine, which put out traps for me at every flick of my rubber fins, I felt the vanity of having conducted myself as a conqueror, a master. I had put — we had put — the great ocean sharks to flight; man was invincible, beneath the water as well as on earth. The legend of man-eating sharks collapsed around me.

Alas, this senseless pride survived in me for only a few weeks. It was dissipated by our first encounter with *Carcharhinus longimanus,* the shark that is the undisputed lord of the tropical oceans. In an earlier book I have recounted in detail the circumstances of this first meeting, which came close to being the last for Frédéric Dumas and myself. On board the *Elie Monnier,* we had harpooned a whale, a *globicephalus,* in the tropical Atlantic, off the coasts of the Cape Verde Islands. Our victim, a toothed cetacean weighing almost a ton, was still struggling at the end of a three-hundred-foot line and the other *globicephali* were swimming around the ship, reluctant to abandon their still-living comrade. And of course, some large sharks began to appear. Our ship was stopped, linked to the whale. Dumas and I went into the water, carrying three-bottle tanks on our backs. I also carried a camera, to film the activity of the whales which still surrounded us. The drama began almost at once.

A scientist has just opened the belly of this mother sand shark, finding it full of almost mature babies. A shark can have twenty or more babies at one time. In spite of their primitive internal organization, sharks have a superior reproduction organism, and it was surprising to learn they also have feelings for their offspring—at least there is built-in protection for the young. The mother shark, after giving birth, will not eat for days in the area where she gave birth, so as not to eat her babies by mistake.

Philippe Cousteau's wife, Jan, pictured here, was an assistant to Doctor Walker when he made this Caesarian operation. She devoted much time to these little babies, and she actually saved them by placing them in a tank where they all survived and were studied for a long time.

On a sandy bottom in the Red Sea, this reef shark with black tips swims in the foreground while Michel Deloire, obviously shooting another shark, holds the camera in the background. The reef shark is a very nervous and excitable type, which we found on several occasions to be quite dangerous.

We had scarcely entered the water and were only fifteen or twenty feet below the surface when we saw Lord Longimanus — or, as we came to call him, the Lord of the Long Arms. He resembled none of the sharks we had met before. His squat, gray-brown silhouette was sharply etched against the clear blue of the water. His head was very round and very large, his pectoral fins enormous and his dorsal fin rounded at its extremities. Both fins and tail were marked at the extremity with a large round white spot. He was preceded by a tiny pilot fish poised just in front of his snout and probably propelled by a pressure wave. Confident — too confident — in ourselves, we dropped the line that still linked us with the ship and swam straight toward him. It was some time — much too long a time — before we realized that the Lord of the Long Arms was drawing us with him into the distance, but was not in the least afraid of our approach. As soon as we realized this, we were seized with an almost paralytic fear and wanted nothing more than to return to our ship. But it was too late. The *Elie Monnier,* still attached to the dying whale, had not been able to follow us and had lost sight of our air bubbles in the general commotion of the sea. She was drifting, far from us. We were out of sight of land and I knew that in this area the sea was almost two miles deep. Two blue sharks, very large but classic in form, came to join our *longimanus* and then the three squali began to dance around us, in a gradually narrowing circle. For twenty seemingly interminable minutes, the three sharks, prudently but resolutely, attempted a bite at us each time we turned our back on them or each time one of us went up to the surface to signal — in vain — to our far-off ship. Miraculously, the gig which the captain of the *Elie Monnier* had put overboard to look for us found us and saved us from imminent death. Shortly before we were hauled from the water I had arrived at the point of smashing my camera against the head of the *longimanus,* in the forlorn hope of warding off his attack and gaining a little time.

This misadventure, which I would judge very severely today, was a result of the excessive confidence in ourselves acquired during the preceding weeks. It was also due to the temperament of the Lord of the Long Arms. Since that time we have encountered hundreds of these roundish sharks with round fins and round spots: they are the only member of their species that is never really afraid of divers.

On several other occasions we have also experienced difficulties with sharks. On the east coast of the volcanic island of Djebel Taïr in the Red Sea, for example, Falco and Dumas were forced to take refuge in a coral grotto to protect themselves from a pack of sharks that seemed to be in the throes of an extraordinary mass frenzy. And in the waters south of this same island of Djebel Taïr, Dumas and I found ourselves in the midst of several dozen small sharks, about three feet in length, who were highly agitated about something and behaved rather like a pack of young wolves. We were forced to leave the water at once. We have discovered, as a matter of fact, that very young sharks are often more disturbing than larger ones. Sometimes they will be seized with a collective panic and flee, but at other times, on the contrary, it is impossible to get rid of them.

In this connection, I remember an incident that took place near the island of Boa Vista in the South Atlantic. We had captured a female tiger shark that was on the point of giving birth. Doctor Longet performed a Caesarean operation on the dying animal and twenty or so perfectly proportioned little tiger sharks were put back in the water. I was in the water at the time myself, carrying a wooden stick I used to scatter the sea urchins from the area where I was working. Without hesitation, one of the newborn sharks seized the stick in its jaws and shook it vigorously, flinging the whole weight of his body into the attack, in perfect imitation of the movement of adults when they are biting off portions of the flesh of wounded dolphins or whales.

It was while thinking of this baby shark biting on a stick and of the camera I had used to ward off the attacks of the *Carcharhinus longimanus* that I decided to provide our divers with what we later termed a "shark billy." This is a simple three-foot shaft of wood, equipped with blunt, non-slip points at one end. Along with the antishark cage, it is still the only protective device of some effectiveness.

Among our collections in the Oceanographic Museum in Monaco, we have some fossilized teeth of a species of shark that has now disappeared — the *Carcharodon megalodon*. These razor-sharp triangular teeth resemble the teeth of the great white "man-eating" shark, the *Carcharodon carcharias,* but they are enormous — ten times larger than those of its contemporary descendant. They suggest a race of super "man-eaters," more than sixty feet in length, which luckily lived in an era long before the appearance of man. Unfortunately, the teeth of this titanic ancestor are all we possess, since the skeletons of sharks, being entirely cartilaginous, leave no trace. It was therefore necessary for our taxidermists to observe the strictest scientific caution in constructing a life-size model of this vanished giant. In his open jaws, he could have swallowed a small truck!

THREE:
The Perfect Killer
The wounded sperm whale and the fury of the open-sea sharks in the Indian Ocean. The shark's perception of pressure waves. The shark's sense of smell. Shark and spearfisherman. The shark's acute sense of vision.

Jacques-Yves Cousteau's narrative continues

Putting men in cages to protect them from sharks is what we have been doing for the past twenty years, since we could not carry out such an operation in reverse, which would have been much more logical. These human zoos, cages of steel or aluminum, are hung beneath the *Calypso,* or even beneath one of the smaller boats, to provide our divers with a shelter in case of need. If all goes well, they do not use them. If relations between men and sharks become strained, the divers retreat toward a cage. If the situation becomes untenable, they enter the cage and give the signal to be brought up to the surface. It is because of these cages that we have been able to observe and film sharks during their most savage orgies of feeding.

The "perfect killer" is equipped with an enormous jaw set with incredibly sharp teeth, with a powerful and efficient means of propulsion, and with very sensitive devices of perception. However, this block of muscles is supported only by the relatively weak cartilaginous skeleton, the jaw is withdrawn be-

Jacques-Yves Cousteau, wearing a funny hat, is directing the reinforcement of a shark cage. From left to right: Serge Foulon, Paul Zuéna, Claude Templier, Jacques-Yves Cousteau, Philippe Cousteau, and Marcel Soudre. Inside the cage can be seen the fish that will serve as bait.

neath the head, the jawbone is lacking in rigidity, and the teeth do not really form a part of it. Can these contradictory characteristics be compatible?

It was not until fifteen years ago, when the *Calypso* became involved in a drama of the high seas, that I was able to observe closely the actual functioning of the killing machine that is a shark. One hundred miles north of the equator, in the middle of the Indian Ocean, the *Calypso* encountered a large number of sperm whales, dispersed in little groups of from three to seven each and moving quite slowly, probably because of the presence of numerous baby whales. We followed them all morning, sometimes very closely, so closely, in fact, that at a speed of only eight knots, we were unable to avoid a collision between the prow of the ship and a large female, probably weighing about twenty tons. Our precious underwater observation chamber was badly dented by the shock, and Louis Malle, who was in the chamber filming the whales, got a rude jolt. We had just gotten under way again when a very young whale, about twelve feet in length and doubtless no more than a few weeks old, crashed into our port propeller. The sharp blades of the propeller sliced into the body of the unfortunate whale like a machine for slicing ham, and he began to bleed profusely. In spite of his wounds he swam off to rejoin his parents, and for some time the group of adults surrounded the little victim of the accident, trying to help and protect him. Then a very large male, probably the leader of the herd, lifted himself vertically out of the water, supporting himself on the violent lashing of his tail, and for several seconds held more than a third of his body above the level of the waves. In this position, he half-turned toward us and we were sure we could read fury in his glittering little eye. The *Calypso* had seriously wounded two of his charges and he seemed to be studying us carefully, weighing the possibility of revenge. But he apparently decided the danger was too great and plunged back into the ocean. The rest of the herd followed him almost at once, disappearing into the depths, leaving the mortally wounded baby behind. We cut short its suffering with a bullet in its head, and then secured it to the line from the crane on the quarterdeck.

It was not very long before the first shark was sighted, then there were two, ten, twenty. They were all *Carcharhinus longimanus,* the long-finned lords of the deep. They ranged in size from eight to twelve feet. They were joined very shortly by a superb blue shark, about fifteen feet in length, with a long, pointed snout, a slender silhouette, and enormous, expressionless eyes. He was a "blue whaler." Just behind their mouths, almost all the sharks carried a half dozen or so remoras, or sucking fish, oddly resembling decorations on the chest of a general, and they were all escorted by a cloud of pilot fish. While the protective cages and the diving and filming material were being prepared, I observed the behavior of the horde of sharks that now surrounded the bleeding whale. Where had these marauders come from, surging out of the immensity of the sea, a hundred and fifty miles from the nearest island, and with almost three miles of water beneath our keel? They had undoubtedly all been satellites of the school of sperm whales, remaining prudently in their wake, respectful of their power, but ready to take advantage of the slightest weakening, and living on the scraps of their meals.

The attitude of the sharks in their first approach was perfectly clear-cut. Carrying prudence to its extremes, they circled around the still-warm carcass of the baby whale, maintaining a constant, almost lazy, speed. But even so, they seemed very sure of themselves. They quite obviously had no fear of us. If we chased one of them away with boat hooks, he returned a moment later. Time was working for them, and they knew it. The prey could not escape them.

For an entire hour these maneuvers continued, and still not a single shark had ventured too close to the little whale. Then they began to touch him with their snouts, barely grazing him, one by one and hundreds of times, but making no attempt to bite. They behaved the same way with our protective cage.

Suddenly, the blue shark lunged and bit. With a single blow, as if from some giant razor, pounds of skin, of flesh, and of fat were sliced away. It was the signal; the orgy was about to begin.

With no apparent transition, the calm of the preliminary round gave way to the frenzy of sharing in the spoils. Each mouthful snatched by each passing shark dug a hole the size of a bucket in the body of the dead whale. I could not believe my eyes. Instinctively, and horrified, I thought of similar scenes which must have taken place after a shipwreck or the crash of a plane into the sea.

Because of the safety afforded by our cage — although it was constantly bumped and jostled by these ravenous beasts — we were able to film their saturnalia in close-up, at a distance of only a few feet. It was as a result of this experience that I learned the mechanism by which a shark bites into his prey.

The shark's jaw is located far back beneath his long snout, but this does not prevent him from biting directly into the flesh. When he opens the jaw, the lower jawbone is thrust forward while the snout is drawn back and up, until it makes almost a right angle with the axis of his body. At this moment, the mouth is located forward of the head and no longer beneath it. It resembles a large wolftrap, equipped with innumerable sharp and gleaming teeth. The shark plants this mechanism in the body of his victim and uses the weight of his own body in a series of frenzied convulsions, transforming the teeth of the jawbones into saws. The force of this sawing effect is such that it requires no more than an instant for a shark to tear off a splendid morsel of flesh. When the shark swims off, he has left a deep and perfectly outlined hole in the body of his victim. It is terrifying and nauseating to watch.

Philippe Cousteau's narrative

One of the mysteries of nature that most highly stimulate the imagination is that of communications. On the surface of the earth, the presence of a predator in a forest is known immediately to all the forest's inhabitants. Vultures and other carrion-eaters appear in the vicinity before an ill or wounded animal

A great blue shark with two pilot fish and remora under his mouth. The shark swims close to the diving ladder at the rear of the *Calypso*. The photographer was hidden between the rudders of the ship to shoot this picture.

has had time to die. In our world of air and light, warnings are provided by sight, scent, and sound, not only to animals but to ourselves. For underwater animals, sight and the sense of smell play simple roles and function more or less as they do on the surface. The same thing is true of the sense of hearing, but in the aquatic world one factor has changed. I think I may say that all marine animals resemble their cousins on the surface of the earth in that they can emit sounds, but they have the unique capability of moving within their liquid element without producing any audible sound. It is this that creates a "silent world." And yet, marine animals, like land animals, have the faculty of foreseeing the arrival, the passing, the absolutely silent attack of one of their own kind. It is this faculty, which I believe to be common to all fish, that I have termed the "comprehension" or the "sensation" of water. Bodies — either more or less solid — moving through a liquid element create what has come to be known as a pressure wave. A pressure wave is similar to the puff of wind felt by a man standing on the street when an automobile passes at high speed. In liquids of feeble density, these pressure waves or zones do not travel very far, just as the wave of air from the automobile is not felt if the man moves a few steps away from its path. On the other hand, the more dense the element the more easily the waves are spread, the greater the distance they travel, and the greater their speed. In the sea, each moving body is surrounded by its own network of pressure waves which vary in relation to every characteristic of this particular body and its movement — its speed, the nature of its flesh, its size, its form, or whatever might serve to identify it. Obviously, the means of detection and interpretation of pressure waves vary greatly with each species of animal and even a highly developed marine mammal such as the dolphin is incapable of determining the origin and cause of the pressure wave he feels on his sensitive skin. Bony fish, on the other hand, can derive from pressure waves all the information necessary to their survival. Although a different system is at work, the same thing is true of the cartilaginous fishes — among them, the shark.

In the case of squali, it is generally admitted that the sensorial system most specifically adapted to detection and interpretation of pressure waves is concentrated in a narrow band which runs along each side of the animal, from the region surrounding the eye to the slender section at the beginning of the tail. This is the "lateral" system, made up of canals running beneath the skin and linked to the outside by minute tubes opening, through the pores, onto the water itself. These canals are filled with a mucous substance which transmits and perhaps even amplifies vibrations, and they are also strewn with finely lidded nerve cells. The movement of the lids on these cells, relative to their normal position of rest, releases a nervous influx which is instantly communicated to the brain. The information thus gathered is then analyzed and determines the reaction of the shark. I have seen sharks appear from behind a bank of rock or coral, moving swiftly, and obviously attracted by violent clapping of the hands, done in an effort to send out strong pressure waves.

Some biologists think that the shark's perception of vibrations, such as pressure waves, is limited to a maximum distance of one hundred feet from their source. The auditory sense, on the other hand, is thought to be far more highly developed and would permit reception of information coming from a much greater distance. I shall return to this subject in chapter 12.

One of the senses of marine animals that most astonish me is that of smell. I have difficulty imagining that odors can be distinguished in water, which is certainly the most neutral of elements. And yet, sharks are capable of following a scent across miles of ocean and arriving precisely at its source. It was probably this faculty which made it possible for them to locate our poor little whale, since the wounds in his body released vast quantities of blood into the sea.

The shark's nostrils are formed in such a manner that his movement through the water creates a continuous current passing over his sensory cells. The nostrils form a kind of furrow in the head, generally running lengthwise or even diagonally to the body, in order to increase the surface of contact between the mucous membrane and the current of water. In those species of sharks that remain motionless at the bottom for long periods of time, the current created by breathing through the mouth is sufficient to cause a circulation of water in the nostrils. Although it is infinitely more sensitive, the olfactory system of squali is based on the same principles as our own. In air, odors are created by suspended particles which are diluted in solution with the mucous matter that covers the interior surface of the nose. It is this chemical solution that excites the olfactory cells. In the marine world, the water itself forms the base of the solution and transports the chemical agents to the cells of the olfactory organ. The fundamental difference and the remarkable particularity of the shark's olfactory system, as compared with ours, lies in the extreme directivity of his response to odors. In most cases, the nostrils of sharks are set very wide apart and can detect differences in the concentration of an odor, causing the shark to turn in the direction of that nostril which has perceived the strongest scent. Moreover, the natural lateral movement of his head while he is swimming permits the nostrils to explore a fairly considerable arc and thus to indicate more precisely the location of the source of the odor. Obviously, the more widely spaced the nostrils the greater the sense of directivity in the olfactory organ; and this has been advanced as one of the possible causes of the strange evolution of the shape of the head of hammerhead sharks *(Sphyrnidae)*. In this particular species, the nostrils are located at the extremity of the lateral protuberances of the head, which in the case of some adult animals can mean a distance of two feet apart.

On board the *Calypso,* we carried out an experiment to study the shark's faculty of directivity and the extreme sensitivity of the olfactory system of squali. We poured a coloring solution of fluorite green onto the flat sand floor of a sixty-foot-deep reef in the Red Sea and followed its course for about a thousand feet. The course of the liquid did not follow a straight line, because of the little eddies and whirlpools formed by the current as it flowed around the obstacles of coral. We marked it with reference points planted in the sand. Then a plastic bag containing the almost colorless liquid extracted from pressed fish was planted at the exact point at which we had poured in the dye marker.

Our wait was of short duration. Two sharks appeared at almost the same time, separated from each other by only a few feet. They were swimming rapidly, seeming impatient, and moving their heads swiftly from left to right. They were followed almost immediately by four others, none of them very large, averaging about three feet in length. All of them skimmed along close to the bottom of clear sand, whose wavelike conformations caused their shadows to vibrate strangely; all were intent on their own pursuit and totally ignored our presence. In the sea, as everywhere else in the natural world, the business of hunger is second in importance only to that of love. As they passed each limb of coral, they seemed a little disoriented and their excitement increased, probably because of the eddies of water which momentarily obscured their trail. In all, however, their search was completed within a distance of less than ten feet from the marked trail and in a time of not more than eight minutes. Seeing these sharks behaving exactly like the dogs of a hunting pack, I remembered the name the Greeks had given them: hounds of the sea.

We conducted this experiment, under simulated conditions, in order to recreate a natural and extremely dangerous situation. When an undersea hunter has caught a fish with his spear gun, he generally removes it from the

The speed capabilities of the porpoise are amazing. This one is breaking surface at high speed, trying to catch up with our ship. Porpoises are capable of maintaining this speed for long periods of time, while the shark can swim as rapidly but only in short bursts.

spear, attaches it to his belt, and goes on with the hunt. In doing so, he leaves behind him a trail of blood and scent emanating from the wounded or dead fish he is carrying at his waistline. If there are any sharks in the area, they will arrive on the scene almost immediately, attracted primarily by the pressure waves set up by the frantic movement of the dying fish. After this, they will pick up the scent of dead fish and trace it to the foolhardy swimmer, thus bringing about another "shark attack," although I know of no fatalities, so far, among Scuba divers.

When one reads through the reports of attacks on imprudent undersea hunters throughout the world, it becomes apparent that all, or almost all of the wounds inflicted by sharks are at the level of the waist, precisely where any dead fish are attached. What renders matters so inevitable under these circumstances is the fact that while a normal diver remains a problem to the shark and incites him to prudence, because of the shark's lack of positive information, an undersea hunter surrounded by the scent of his catch becomes a natural prey to the unhesitating shark. In full consciousness of the risk they are taking, certain devotees of the aquatic massacre they term sport attach their captives to a length of cord which they then trail at a distance of fifteen to twenty feet behind them. And, as a rule, they survive unhurt from the attacks of sharks.

In his fine book, *Shark Attack,* V. M. Coppleson writes: "Most injuries to skin divers have been caused by sharks robbing them of fish. Spearfishermen holding fish should never be surprised to find they have a shark for a companion." Among our crew, of course, there is no question of such imprudence, and if by chance we have decided to spear a fish for study purposes or to give a change to our menu, the hunter surfaces as soon as the fish is speared, and passes the entire gun to the companion in the small boat which has accompanied him. If he sees any sign of sharks in the area, he leaves the water at once.

One of the most tenacious of the legends circulated with regard to sharks is the one which claims that he has poor eyesight. Like all such information with no basis in truth, this legend is dangerous, since the unwarned diver may allow a shark to approach, in the hope of going unobserved. Our experience on the *Calypso* has been considerably different. One day, for example, when I went into the water on a shallow reef off the coast of Africa, near the Cape Verde Islands, I sighted a shark at a considerable distance from me. I could scarcely make him out, and was only able to do so because his grayish color was silhouetted very clearly against the dazzling whiteness of the sand. At that particular moment, I was floating at a very shallow depth, without making any movement, so that the sound of bubbles from my aqualung would be confused with the light splashing of the water. I turned my eyes away for a few seconds, to study the symmetrical design of a giant ray just beneath me, which had half-covered itself with sand, as rays often do in an effort to make themselves invisible. I am not sure now whether it was simple instinct or a perception of movement, but I turned back abruptly toward the location of the shark. And immediately, every muscle of my body tensed. He was no more than thirty feet away and was launched toward me as hard and swift as a missile. My hands held no protective device and I was alone. The sight of a shark coming at you head-on is very strange, and obviously it is from that angle that he seems most formidable. The eyes are almost invisible, because of their lateral positioning, while the slit in the half-opened mouth, and the three regularly spaced fins give him the appearance of a malignant and terrifying symbol imagined by some Aztec sorcerer. When he had approached to within two feet of the rubber fins I had hurled at him as a futile gesture of protection, the shark turned suddenly and swam back toward the depths.

From a full-face angle, you can see that the shark has lost most of his grace and beauty. He is just a mean-looking, dangerous killer.

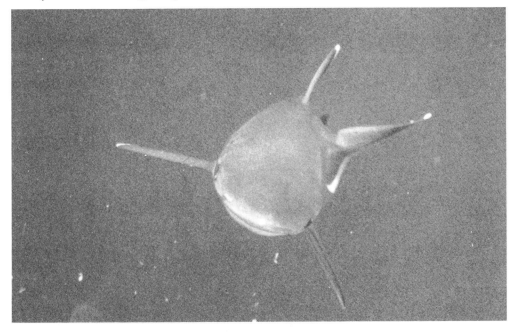

I must admit that I did not think to identify his species, but he must have measured seven to ten feet in length.

There had been no sound, no scent, and it appears certain that sight was the sense responsible for this attack. Professor Perry W. Gilbert, after having studied the visual processes of twenty or so sharks, arrived at the following conclusions: the retina of the shark's eye is extremely rich in rods and relatively poor in cones, which would imply a great sensitivity to light but a relatively small power of resolution and perception of colors. To increase the sensitivity of the system, silvery plates, or tapetum, placed behind the retina, reflect light back through the retina, allowing it to be stimulated twice by the same ray of light. To protect the eye from an extremely bright light, a membraneous surface of pigmented cells can extend to cover the silvery plates and render them inoperative. The pupil is highly mobile and can be closed to an extreme degree, so that it no longer forms anything more than a tiny point or a slit, according to the different species of shark. The crystalline lens, which is almost spherical and cannot change shape, has a high refractive index, and in its rest position, provides a sharp image of objects in the far distance. To focus on nearer objects, the muscles attached to the lens thrust it forward, without altering its shape. The shark is thus perfectly equipped to see at a distance and to distinguish among forms, especially if they produce a contrast in luminous intensity with the light surrounding them. The high degree of sensitivity of the shark's eye also makes it an excellent organ of perception in very feeble light.

In the experience I have mentioned, the shark was beneath me and my body was clearly silhouetted against the harsh light of the surface, so all conditions were favorable to him.

All these attributes, these unique characteristics, and still others, which I will describe in the course of our accounts of later confrontations, make of the shark a terribly efficient predator. In his own kingdom, he seems invincible and, in fact, he very nearly is — or rather, he was, for a period of millions of years, until his universe was invaded by warm-blooded animals, the cetaceans. It was only these superior beings that brought about the defeat of the shark. On the surface of the earth, great reptiles weighing tens of tons were exterminated by relatively tiny mammals. In the marine world, there was no extermination, but simply the appearance of a superior intelligence and a greater power of adaptation. And with this, the shark was despoiled of his invincibility.

FOUR:
Warm Blood and Cold Blood

What happened to a wounded dolphin out in the sea. The shark follows dolphins or other herds of sea mammals. A shark killed by dolphins in an aquarium. How sharks feed on whales.

Philippe Cousteau's narrative continues

A sunrise, the changing pattern of waves on a beach, a snowfall, a star-studded sky — these are daily spectacles, and yet I never tire of them. For me, dreams emerge as much from contemplation as from the most decisive form of action, and the magnificent disorder of a universe governed by chance and through the medium of ephemeral and changing laws becomes a familiar thing. In the course of these marvelous wanderings of the mind, the vain desire to understand it all vanishes, leaving behind only an instinctive exaltation and joy. And there is no vision which draws me toward these carefree reveries quite so strongly as the sight of a group of dolphins playing in the waters at the prow of a ship.

When the group is numerous, they seem to arrive from every direction at once. Those who come from behind swim with all their strength and speed, following the line of waves tossed up and out by the prow. They spring up almost horizontally from the outermost flank of the wave and plunge back, just beneath the surface, at the precise spot where the displacement of water is most favorable to them. When they arrive forward of the ship their movement is slower and they will circle about in an impeccable pirouette, waiting for the proper moment to place themselves within a few inches of the prow, where the pressure wave created by the ship assures them of a maximum of thrust. Then the game really begins. They swim simply, their sihouettes slightly blurred by the streaming flow of water, skimming its surface in quest of a few rapid breaths of air. Like the best competitive swimmers, they limit their breathing periods as much as possible, exhaling beneath the water and creating a string of silvery bubbles spurting up from time to time from the blowhole in their heads. These underwater exhalations are also signs of excited conversations among the playful dolphins, as the air forced through the more or less tightly closed blowholes produces vibrations that the animal modulates and uses to communicate with the others. The best places for their game, in the hollow of the wave just in front of the prow, are scarce, so each member of the team takes his turn at occupying one of them. From the observation chamber beneath the forward section of the *Calypso's* hull, the spectacle seems unreal. In conjunction with the displacement of water by the ship, they appear almost motionless, propelled by some magical force. All the movements of acrobatics form a part of their repertoire: spins and somersaults, vertical plunges or leaps above the water. Sometimes they allow themselves to be pushed along by the vessel, almost matching their tail to the roundness of the bow; they will remain absolutely motionless, conforming perfectly to the axis of the ship's movement, driven through the water by the thousand horsepower of our diesel engines and expending no effort to propel themselves but only to hold on. The youngest among them are permitted only very brief periods at this game, always accompanied by their mother, swimming close beside them, either from simple caution or because the strength of the children does not allow them the effort of maintaining the precarious and tiring position for any length of time. I have never seen a baby dolphin join the play by himself; it would seem that this is forbidden. All of them watch us closely through the screen of water and glass, and their laughing eyes seem to be waiting for encouragement or applause. It is the warmth and gaiety of their regard that attracts me most. I have seen the ship's doctor perform an "autopsy" on a female found ill and dying off the coast of the island of Stromboli in the Mediterranean. Since he had not succeeded in curing her, he decided to study the body, in an attempt to discover the reasons for her illness — which turned out to be a ruptured intestine. During the whole of the operation he did not speak a word, and his face wore an expression of gravity which revealed his emotions. The anatomy of the dolphin is so close to our own that the analogy was haunting him.

Dolphins are mammals, just as we are, and like us their blood is warm. The size, the weight, and the number of convolutions of their brain are closely related to ours, and the same thing is true of their other organs. Because of their internal system, dolphins are fragile animals, far more so than fish or squali. But their adaptation to the sea has been no less complete or efficient. Like the sharks, they have attained a hydrodynamic state of near-perfection. Both are capable of almost the same speed in short sprints and both are widely represented in all the seas of the globe. Their nourishment is the same, based on fish, but there is one difference: the dolphin does not eat meat, while the shark occasionally does. And this is what has made them enemies. Two rival lords cannot share the same domain, and inevitably one must dominate the other. Here, the fundamental difference lies in the fact that the shark, feeding on meat, represents a natural threat to the dolphin, while the latter represents none to the squalus, whose flesh does not interest him. Once, for the first time, certainly millions of years before man, a hungry shark must have attacked a dolphin. We can imagine that the shark was the victor in this original combat, and as occurred in biblical history, he became the marine incarnation of evil. The analogy with the biblical story of creation ends here, since the shark, although he remains the Cain of the aquatic world in the minds of most men, has not been so fortunate in his feudal realm as the descendants of Abel's brother have been in ours.

Paradoxically, the transformations undergone by the dolphin in successfully adapting himself to marine life have in no way weakened or bothered him. On the contrary, the vertebral column of a land animal has given him a more efficient vertical swimming movement, especially for an animal that breathes on the surface. His smooth skin, distended by fat, facilitates and even controls the flow of water around him (the laminar stream), and reduces resistance to his forward movement to a minimum. And lastly, the fact of being a warm-blooded animal makes possible a far more prolonged muscular effort than that of any fish, including the shark. In mammals, the blood circulates more rapidly and under greater pressure than in cold-blooded fish. Consequently, since the quantity of oxygenated blood which reaches the muscles of warm-blooded animals is greater, so too the effectiveness of the

The porpoise in the foreground is racing with our launch, the *Zodiac*. The *Zodiac* has a forty-horsepower engine, and it is here traveling at a speed in excess of twenty knots. The porpoise, by the mere fact that he is jumping high out of the water, shows that he is just playing and not really giving his all.

muscular tissues is greater. In sum, although the dolphin and the shark are capable of comparable bursts of speed over a short distance, the dolphin can maintain this speed for a considerably longer period of time. In passing, I might mention that the greatest speed measured for a dolphin is close to thirty knots but this might not be his maximum speed in the event of danger. Moreover, this speed may vary according to species and there are a dozen different species of dolphins.

Another fundamental difference — and this one to the shark's advantage — is the disproportion between their jaws. The jaw of the shark is formidably equipped with teeth which are both sharp and pointed, capable of cutting across the bone as well as into the flesh, and opening into a mouth of impressive size. The dolphin's mouth, on the other hand, carries only small, pointed teeth, inclined to the rear, adapted to catch and hold on to a fish, but not to cut or to tear apart. And yet, it is this jaw of the dolphin which constitutes his principal weapon of both attack and defense against the shark. We shall discuss the mechanics of this on pages 53-56.

Finally, the principal advantage of the dolphin is his superior intelligence and the ability he has developed of communicating with his fellows. The shark is a solitary beast, resembling in this sense some Alaskan wolves. His association with others of his own race is only occasional and never planned. When it does occur, it is primarily at moments of a division of spoils. The dolphin, on the contrary, lives in very highly organized groups, capable of inventing and applying a single strategy for the entire group. I have often noticed, however, that the groups of dolphins cruising the high seas are always followed, a few hours later, by several large sharks. We must, therefore, imagine that the squali find what they are looking for; but how? I doubt that anyone really knows, but perhaps things happen thus:

Twilight on the ocean is always a mystical ballet, grave and true as no other spectacle can be. It is a changing of values so profound, so complete that everyone, man or beast, experiences it in the very depths of his being. In the vast liquid space, threaded with changing vibrations, the troop of dolphins slows down and gathers more closely together, as does every band of nomads when night approaches. On the long flat swell, the crests of waves take on a roseate color, a bloody presage for the troop, since the night often assumes the countenance of death. Little cries and warnings are called back and forth in the sharp rhythm of trills and chatterings proper to their language. The ranks close up, and the young take their place near the dorsal fin of their mother. A trifle farther out, the males form the protective circle. And a mile away, the sharks also change formation. Forewarned by the waning of the light and by their obscure millenary instinct, they too move more closely together. The purplish rippling of the last rays of sun mingles with the thin, steely furrows plowed by the tail and the triangular fins. Night is now complete, and the dolphins are sleeping. A few inches beneath the surface, they return to it every half minute, still sleeping, to breathe its cold and humid air. The young regulate their breathing on that of their mother, jealously guarding the favored position just to the rear of the dorsal fin. All of the troop frequently opens its eyes to the silver-studded velvet of night at sea.

At night, because of the evaporation caused by the rays of the sun during the day, the air on the surface of the sea seems colder while the water, in contrast, seems tepid and restful. A solitary dolphin has allowed himself to drift from the immediate proximity of the group. His sleep, which is generally interrupted every few minutes, is deeper than normal. And yet, those moments of wakefulness required to resume his place in the formation are often vital. Is he an old soldier more fatigued by the long day's journey than he has ever been before? Or a carefree youth lingering for a last frolic among the slopes of the evening swell? Or perhaps just a sick dolphin, whose sleep is already eternal?

The silvery eye of a great blue shark picks out the still, black form, and when it is a matter of the pursuit of a solitary prey there is no hesitancy in his reaction; he attacks.

From the shattered chest of the dolphin, a great black bubble of air carries away his own life and, with it, the last warning he will ever convey to his fellows. The rest of the troop, instantly alert but blinded by the night, can only listen to the sounds of the pack of sharks which now accompanies the dead dolphin as he sinks toward the abyss in an apotheosis of pale phosphorescence. The sea resounds with sharp, short cries. These are the signals sent out by the other dolphins, and in listening for their echo they learn the location of the enemy, the prey, or the friend. Thanks to this echo-sounding apparatus, which pierces the darkness around them, they now know that the danger is past, the pack is far beneath them and probably satiated. The night again is calm, disturbed only by the frenetic ballet of the luminous micro-organisms constantly tracing out their web of ephemeral light.

I do not think that every night brings such tragic consequences for the dolphins. In fact, sharks follow the troop primarily to secure food from the bodies of ill or wounded animals left behind, from babies born dead, and even from morsels of the umbilical cord or the matrix rejected after a birth. Accidents such as those I have described above must be rare, and I have myself seen sharks flee from dolphins.

It was in the Red Sea, along a coral barrier on the western edge of the Farasan Islands off lower Saudi Arabia. In the crystal-clear water, dotted with busy fish, my attention was suddenly drawn to an abrupt and unexpected movement. A shark of respectable size shot by me like an arrow, clearly in bewildered flight and closely followed by two dolphins. Just as they were about to disappear in the distance, I could distinguish two other forms arriving from the opposite direction and forcing the shark to turn ninety degrees to his left. He vanished in the direction of the open sea, still followed by the now-united group of four dolphins. I had the impression of witnessing one of the cruel games of the sea, and this time it was the shark who was its scapegoat. I do not know how this particular hunting party ended, but if I am to go by the studies made at Marineland of the Pacific, the big California aquarium, I can only conclude that it was not in a victory for the shark.

The events I am about to relate took place in several aquariums in the United States, and form the basis of my contention that the shark, although he represents a constant threat to the dolphin, can nonetheless be defeated and held at bay. In one large tank containing several female and some male dolphins, a shark had been living for weeks in seemingly peaceful co-existence. The shark spent all his time swimming along the bottom and eating regularly the food given to him by the aquarium personnel. The dolphins played among themselves and occupied the entire space of the tank, paying no attention to the shark. Then, when one of the female dolphins arrived at the end of her time of pregnancy and was about to give birth, this well-established routine changed abruptly. Either the dolphins had suddenly had enough of the presence of a stranger in their midst or — and this is more likely — they were aware of the danger of giving birth to an infant while this ancestral enemy, so highly sensitive to the smell of blood, was still about. In any event, they decided to rid themselves of him.

Taking their point of departure at the far end of the tank and moving with all the speed of which they were capable, the dolphins took turns at smashing the point of their muzzle against the abdominal cavity of the panicky shark.

This porpoise is breaking the water so rapidly that even with our camera's very high shutter speed he is slightly blurred. He is gaining on the ship, with his back way out of the water, showing here, too, that he is not really giving all he can. It is partly because of their speed that porpoises can do away with sharks with relative ease.

After a few minutes of this performance, the shark was dead. His body bore no visible wounds, but his entrails had been ruptured as thoroughly as if he had been struck with a battering ram.

On another occasion, dolphins rid themselves of a shark, which had been placed in their tank, with such violence that his body was found the next morning at a distance of almost thirty feet from the pool. He had been "thrown overboard," so to speak, and no one could tell whether he was already dead at the time or had died later of asphyxiation.

Making use of their echo-sounding apparatus, their speed, their pointed "beak," and especially of their intelligence, dolphins can hold sharks at bay most of the time, but this is not the case with all cetaceans. Whalers returning from their hunting trips have often brought back horrible tales of enormous packs of sharks attacking whales and tearing them to pieces. These must, however, be relatively rare cases, since the strength of the larger cetaceans is sufficient to crush any form of squali. They may perhaps have been instances of ill or weakened solitary whales, or even of animals mortally wounded by the whalers themselves, or by their natural enemy, the killer whale.

There is no real evidence of any such concerted action on the part of sharks, and it is only the smell of food, blood, or debris which can unleash a massive attack. Obviously, if such an attack does occur, there are very few things capable of resisting it. But, generally, everything takes place as if nature, frightened by the weapons she has herself furnished to sharks, attempts to counterbalance them through a deficient sense of aggression and the absence of a collective intelligence.

Every year, however, sharks mass in large numbers at the entrance to the lagoons of Lower California, to await the migration of the gray whales. In December, regularly, the gray whales migrate from the Arctic to the coasts of Mexico. There, the mothers give birth and raise their young, until the month of March, when they return to the Arctic Ocean. As is true of all wild species, there is a mortality rate of approximately 30 per cent, either at birth or in the weeks that follow. The gray whale, a small species of baleen whale, reaches a size of sixty to sixty-five feet at a maximum. The females give birth, in remote branches of the lagoons, to a single infant (or, rarely, two), weighing about a ton. They then nurse the baby for three to four months.

During one expedition in this area, our research team was guided by Professor Theodore Walker of the Scripps Institute in San Diego. The preceding year he had seen many sharks, one of which had been identified as a white shark (*Carcharodon carcharias*) from a photograph the professor had taken. From our own observations, we had believed that sharks do not penetrate very far into the disturbed and relatively shallow waters of lagoons, and in all my dives in this area I never saw one. One day, however, as Michel Deloire, Professor Walker, and I were exploring one of the interior creeks of Scammon's Lagoon, we found evidence of their presence. A young, dead whale had been left stranded on a beach by the receding tide. I was overcome by a feeling of sadness and melancholy at the sight of this animal who had died without ever having lived, lying there now, an easy prey to the sea birds, in the midst of this landscape of dunes stretching off as far as the eye could see, engulfed in silence, a powerful marine creature destined to be nothing more than carrion. He had probably died of some illness, but on his flanks he bore the sharp, oval marks of the jaws of sharks.

What is astonishing in the case of the gray whales is the fact that the sharks know at what time of year they migrate, and consequently gather together to await them. I do not believe, however, that whale flesh, any more than that of dolphins, forms a regular part of the shark's food. It seems to me more likely that it is simply the expectation of some debris, the remains of a birth, perhaps, borne out by the tide, which causes them to linger around the passages leading into the lagoons. In a sense, it is something like a famished dog waiting for the moment when the cook will bring the garbage through the door of the kitchen.

One species of cetacean combines all the advantages of the dolphin and is also armed with a jaw even more formidable than that of the shark. This is the killer whale, whose power and ability to combine his actions with those of other members of his race are so great that he can defeat even the largest whales of other species — although the adult killer whale measures only between fifteen and twenty-five feet in length. This superiority is amply demonstrated in an account of a spectacle witnessed by Professor Walker. As he was surveying the migration of gray whales from a Coast Guard helicopter, he saw a group of killer whales, along the coast of Lower California, apparently just playing on the surface of the water. A half mile away, a nine- or ten-foot shark was also swimming lazily on the surface. Suddenly, Professor Walker saw one of the whales plunge vertically into the sea and disappear. About three minutes later, the whale shot up just beneath the shark and leaped clear of the water, holding the shark crosswise in his mouth. The two forms seemed suspended in air for a fraction of a second, and then dis-

The *Calypso* at night, sailing the very calm Red Sea.

appeared in a shower of spray. The explanation Professor Walker gives to this extraordinary sequence of events is that the killer whale (*Orcinus orca*) had detected the presence of the shark through its echo-sounding apparatus, despite the distance that separated them. Plunging vertically, he had made his approach at a great depth and then raced to the surface, again vertically, thus taking his prey completely by surprise. A vertical attack from the depths is the last thing a shark might expect.

Thus, the shark is not infallible and in the marine world, as in our own, intelligence and subtlety can win over brute force — if not always, at least quite often. And in the battle between warm blood and cold, it is the mammal that triumphs over the fish. The shark is not the uncontested lord of the deep, but he is certainly the most widely prevalent and most dangerous creature of the sea to another race of warm-blooded mammals: man.

FIVE:
The Squaloscope
Abu Marina.
Operation "la Balue."
The capture and study
of sharks.
Study of anesthetics: cognac,
MS-222.
The respiratory system.

Philippe Cousteau's narrative continues

Canoë (Raymond Kientzy, one of our two chief divers) woke me very early this morning. We were in the Red Sea, in sight of the reefs of Abu Marina.* Together we climbed to the very top of the mast on the upper deck to select the best possible anchorage for the *Calypso*. The spectacle of the vast labyrinth of reefs (most of them barely at the level of the water), of deep channels, and little islands of white sand, made us oddly quiet and thoughtful. It resembled a giant artist's palette, covered with every variation of blues and greens. In these waters we were about to carry out all kinds of experiments and observations on sharks in captivity.

The succession of coral peaks and deep-water inlets extends over an area of several square miles. The average depth of the water within this area is about 200 feet. Our past experiences had shown us that it is often on the exterior borders of these reefs that one finds the most life. Over where the last reef plunged vertically to a depth of 2500 feet, the wild animals of the open sea came in to swell the life surrounding the reef itself. The hunting is better there; it is the privileged domain of the great predators. Sharks cruise

*In the Suakin group, off the coast of Sudan.

Inside the plastic cage called la Balue, Marcel Soudre is floating as if in a bubble. Of course, because of their transparency, the plastic domes that protrude at every side except the bottom of this cage are barely visible, but they are extremely resistant.

here constantly, accompanied by barracuda, great tunas, and schools of silvery fish of the caranx species. It is along this ledge between the open sea and the small, highly colored world of the reef that life becomes more active, and also more violent.

We decided to anchor the *Calypso* very close to the reef, on the eastern side of its outer border, toward the sea. The sonar showed us a bank of sand about sixty-five feet wide and slanting down in a gentle slope. Its depth was about forty-five feet at its highest point against the coral wall, and reached eighty-five feet at the edge of the deep-water area.

As soon as the motors were stopped, a diving team — Canoë and Serge Foulon — went into the water to explore the reef and find the most favorable spot for our installations. A few minutes later they returned and directed us toward a kind of passageway between two coral peaks. On either side, magnificent clumps of multi-colored coral rose to the surface, surrounded by clouds of gleaming, busy little fish. And on every side, the slope inclined gently toward the blue depths. Large species of caranx and schools of surgeonfish seemed to flow in an uninterrupted stream through this miniature Gibraltar.

Is was a perfect spot and our first mate, Paul Zuéna, brought the *Calypso* broadside to the axis of the passage at a distance of about sixty feet from the reefs. The device we planned to use here was a cage six and a half feet tall and four feet wide, with sides formed of domes of transparent plexiglass, highly resistant to shocks. The entire cage was pierced with small openings, designed to allow water to flow into the interior, where the diver was situated. The occupant of this strange apparatus — in this first experiment, it was Marcel Soudre — could either film what was happening outside through the

The structure seen in the background is called a squaloscope—a cage used to house sharks. It was designed by Philippe Cousteau's brother, Jean-Michel, as a means of trapping sharks in order to study their behavior in a confined environment. The roof of the cage is made out of the same kind of domes used in la Balue. In the foreground swims a black-tip reef shark. You can see about five sharks in the picture, but fifty more are swimming around.

transparent walls, move outside himself through a trap door cut into the flooring, or simply observe the behavior of the sharks from a place of complete security. Moreover, this cage, which was designed by my brother, Jean-Michel, and named by him "la Balue" in honor of the unfortunate Cardinal la Balue who was rumored to have been imprisoned in an oversized bird cage by Louis XI, also allowed us to determine whether a diver might be subject to direct attack by sharks. Lastly, when it was turned on its side and the door left open, it made an excellent trap for the capture and study of medium-sized sharks.

With my camera focused toward the surface, I filmed la Balue as it was lowered into the water, which was so clear that I could easily make out the 130-foot length of the *Calypso's* hull. No sooner was la Balue completely submerged than Marcel swam down and into it and released the cable linking it to the ship. It floated gently down, like some majestic soap bubble, visible primarily because of its aluminum uprights and frame. The current was running in toward the passage and lifted the cage slowly toward the summit of the slope. A few small sharks with black-tipped fins had already left the vicinity of the bottom and were mounting toward the cage. They were no more than three feet long and seemed extremely prudent. They circled once or twice around la Balue and then went back down to their lazy evolutions close to the sandbank. It is a rare thing to see these sharks leave the immediate proximity of the bottom or that of a bank of coral, but they can also become dangerous because they are often less cautious than other species and more easily excited. They are the only sharks I have ever seen bite at a prey on first passing it. Marcel, in his plexiglass bubble, was also well aware of this, so he had stopped watching me and was now attentively surveying the sharks.

At last, la Balue touched bottom and I began the descent toward her, filming a long traveling shot. I had emptied my lungs, and I sank down in a completely motionless state, headfirst, and with the camera forming a prolongation of my body. Sucking in air in little mouthfuls, I was experiencing once again the pure joy of movement in three dimensions. When I arrived at the level of the cage, Marcel had already turned it over, so that it was resting horizontally on one of its convex sides. The trap door was open and Marcel had opened a sack containing pieces of fresh fish. I propped myself against a bank of coral and watched, preparing to film. Almost immediately, one of the little sharks snatched the head of a caranx and fled. He was followed instantly by two others and there was a short struggle for possession of the bit of fish. The matter was settled abruptly when the first shark took it on himself to swallow the entire piece at one gulp. The others turned away and the first swam off into the distance, his mouth still open and his head jerking back and forth in a series of brutal convulsions. Then began the race to divide up whatever other spoils there might be. The first incident had brought an additional fifteen or more sharks to the scene, all of the same species and none much longer than about four feet. I pulled back a trifle farther into my coral hiding place and Marcel was forced to close the trap door more and more often, as the sharks' circling became more frequent and more rapid. I noticed that if a shark snatched up a tender bit of the fish flesh and bit into it, there was no consequent frenzy of jealousy and pursuit; but if, on the other hand, it was a bony fragment or a head, the tumult began at once. The sound of teeth grating against bone or even the crunching sound when a shark bites into and crushes a fish head probably constitutes a clear call to any other sharks in the area. Now, the action surrounding the cage had become violent and disordered. Several times I saw a shark crash into the transparent plexiglass and turn away in bewilderment. I do not think they were attempting to get at the diver inside, but only to reach the sack of fish. Every time this happened, I saw Marcel automatically react defensively, holding out his hands and moving toward the back of the cage. It was comical, but perfectly natural. If the shark could not see the obstacle between him and his prey, so too the diver had to become accustomed to not seeing the plastic that protected him.

These mad onslaughts of hordes of sharks toward the precise point where one of their own kind has devoured a bit of fish are terrifying things to watch. They give the impression of being completely unstoppable and fatal. Once, when I was diving with Canoë on the sunny slope of a little reef in the Red Sea, we came very close to becoming victims of this same phenomenon. We had speared a caranx, but since the wound was not mortal, he was struggling fiercely at the end of the line. A long shark with white fins appeared almost at once and began cruising around just outside the little fault in the rock in which we were partially sheltered. It became a matter of urgency to finish off our fish before his movement attracted the shark too close. Canoë therefore pulled out his diver's knife and plunged it into the caranx's head, piercing the bone and destroying the nerve centers. I saw the big shark turn, so quickly that his movement was no more than a blur. He covered the few feet separating him from us at fantastic speed and hurled himself violently against the air tanks on my partner's back. Then, apparently stunned a little, he turned again and swam away as fast as he had arrived. Neither Canoë nor I had had time to make a move, but fortunately my friend, protected by his aqualung, was uninjured. I think that what brought on this lightning attack was a combination of the sound of the knife piercing bone and a last jerking movement of our poor victim. There can be no doubt that sharks hear perfectly, and experience has shown that they react to the sound of blows under water, to the sound of a bell, or to the noises made by a diver at work. In general, their reaction is one of intense interest, and bits of advice in the manner of: "If you see a shark approaching, beat the water with your hands," or the famous warning given to beginning divers, "If you want to drive a shark away, cry out in the water," are little short of criminal. I have often tried the two methods I have just mentioned and at best they have shown no results other than giving me a severe case of laryngitis or sorely bruised hands. In the majority of cases, the immediate consequence of a blow of the palm against the water or a shout was an immediate attack. Often, during dives made for the purpose of studying or filming sharks, we have used the method of calling out beneath the water, not to drive them away, but precisely to attract them into the range of the camera.

Another of our instruments is the "squaloscope," conceived and designed by my brother, Jean-Michel, to serve as an enclosure for the observation and study of sharks in a confined area. It is a rectangular box, twelve feet by nine, and three feet high, with sides formed of vertical bars placed about six inches apart. The roof is composed of four transparent plastic domes, making it possible to observe the sharks that are inside the squaloscope. There is no bottom to it, and one of the sides is divided into two sections and provided with a plastic slab which moves in slots to form the door.

We had put it in place that same morning, and a large distribution of fish from the ship contributed to attracting sharks to the area where we were working. Paul Zuéna, our first mate, had dropped the squaloscope to the level of the water, alongside the hull. Since the air imprisoned in the plastic domes sufficed to keep the whole thing afloat, it was a very simple matter to tow it into position directly above any site we had chosen to work in. When we "uncorked" the aperture in the peak of each dome, the air escaped, water flowed in, and the squaloscope fell as gracefully as an autumn leaf, to come to rest on the sandbank sixty feet below.

We had adopted the technique of "bodyguards," which meant that we dived in teams of two men each, and one of these was responsible only for protecting the back of the other. The first group was made up of Canoë and José Ruiz. I was in charge of the camera, with Serge Foulon as my bodyguard. At the very first glance, I could make out a good twenty or more sharks. Many of them were reef sharks, with black fins and measuring about four feet at most, but among them were several larger sharks with fins bordered in white. These were *Albimarginatus*, definitely more disquieting than the others. They made me think of tigers in the midst of a brood of domestic cats.

They had already begun their lazy circling, studying the squaloscope with their expressionless eyes. Some of them swam up, as if to meet us, but

A shark is following a sliver of fish that is being pulled into the squaloscope. The diver in the background will immediately close the door, rendering the shark captive. Amazingly enough, when the shark entered the cage, although he was about to get the prey he instantaneously forgot his goal and busied himself only with a means of getting out. He started circling excitedly. The other sharks around show the first signs of frenzy, which can become dangerous, especially with the one at the left coming straight at the camera.

This is back-to-back protection, employed when there are several sharks in open water. This white-tip reef shark is kept away by the diver facing us, with the help of the short stick in his right hand pointing at the shark. The back-to-back position is applied when there is no reef nearby or vertical cliffs, or anything, to protect the 180 degrees your sight cannot cover; the back is, of course, almost as vulnerable as the front. By this means, the divers can protect each other very efficiently.

when they had come only halfway they turned abruptly and went back down toward the bottom. Sometimes this procedure can become dangerous to divers. It seems that if one shark is swimming a trifle fast, the others sense his haste and rush to move ahead of him. Although it never occurs with the larger sharks, one often sees four or five small ones approaching at fantastic speed, ready to bite without hesitation.

Canoë set to work putting in place the apparatus we had devised for capturing the sharks. Through the bars of the side of the squaloscope opposite the door, he passed a hemp rope bearing at one end an unbarbed fishhook planted in a morsel of fresh fish. This rope extended across the cage and through the door, with the bait left just outside. When a shark found the piece of fish and lunged for it, Canoë would quickly withdraw the rope, and if the shark followed the bait inside the squaloscope, the door would close behind him. It is an extremely simple process when applied to rabbits or mice, but when it is carried out by four divers sixty feet beneath the surface on a reef in the Red Sea and surrounded by a pack of more than twenty-five sharks, it is quite a different matter.

Things became confused very quickly, and the rhythm of events accelerated. Canoë and José succeeded in getting two sharks into the squaloscope at once, but by this time the scent of fresh fish was acting on all the others like smoke on a beehive. While José was putting the bait back in place, I saw two fairly small sharks crash against the framework of the cage and rebound like ricocheting bullets. The water around us was streaked with gray silhouettes flashing by in every direction. It became difficult to see everything that was happening. A six-foot shark bit into the bait and so fiercely battled Canoë's attempts to pull him into the squaloscope that the whole cage trembled. The man on one end of the rope and the shark at the other pulled with all their strength, until the shark succeeded in wedging himself against a corner of the squaloscope and broke the rope. Out of the corner of my eye I saw José ridding himself of the sack of fish he was carrying in his hands; a small shark opened an enormous mouth and swallowed the whole thing, sack and all. Canoë beat off one of the big *Albimarginatus* with blows of his fists and started toward the surface. At this moment I felt a shock against my left leg and saw a four-foot shark sweep by. He had brushed me with his snout, but fortunately he had not taken a bite. Gathering together in a tight little group, each of us surveying one sector of the area around us and lashing out with shark billies and cameras, we swam back up to the boat, still surrounded by a carrousel of gray arrows, enormously powerful but completely unorganized.

I think it is the irrationality in this frenzy of sharks that strikes me most. It gives me a feeling of complete impotence, such as I never experience in any other circumstances. The shark is the most mechanical animal I know, and his attacks are totally senseless. Sometimes he will flee from a naked and unarmed diver, and at other times he will hurl himself against a steel cage and bite furiously at the bars.

With any other animal, I know that my actions or reactions have a direct influence on its behavior. A crow will fly away if I walk through the fields carrying a stick, since he knows that it might be a rifle. A dog reacts if he senses that someone is afraid of him, and even the fish along the coasts of France are more tame when a diver is not carrying a spear gun. The shark moves through my universe like a marionette whose strings are controlled by someone other than the power manipulating mine; he seems to come from another planet, and in fact he does come from another time. He has not evolved since his beginning, more than a hundred million years ago; he is still in his original state of disorganization. His actions have no logic and are not even natural, and yet he is perfectly adapted to his life. Or perhaps the reverse is true and his order, his logic, are simply not the same as mine. There do, after all, exist intelligences just as different from ours quite near to us — those of insects, for example.

We climbed back on board the *Calypso* still dazed, silent, imbued with an emotion that was neither fear nor apprehension for the future. We felt no sense of relief at having — all of us — escaped from imminent peril, and yet we were exhausted, vaguely conscious of having passed through an exceptional experience. I remembered the shock I had felt against my left knee and could not help but wonder by what chance I had not been bitten.

This habit sharks have of bumping against strange objects floating on the waters has been the subject of intensive study. Professor Budker, in particular, has concluded that squali can taste objects through the use of "sensorial crypts" dissimulated beneath the peculiar scales of the shark's skin. These sensorial crypts are constituted in a manner similar to that of the gustatory papillae, and although they do not react to the same chemical substances, they are linked by their nerve fibers to the same nerve as that which controls the papillae of the mouth and the pharynx. Thus, sharks can obtain information on the taste of a potential prey by rubbing their skin against it. Either because the water in the immediate vicinity of the prey is charged with revealing chemical substances, or because the abrasive skin of the shark detaches a sufficient number of particles of matter to cause a reaction in the nerve terminals of the crypts, the hunter is immediately informed as to the nature of the object he has rubbed against. It was probably the disagreeable flavor of my neoprene-rubber diving suit to which I owe the fact that I still have two legs.

That afternoon we went down again, but this time the big steel cage went with us. Now, in case of necessity, we would not have to fear the dangerous moments of a slow climb to the surface, when we would be deprived of the protection offered by the floor of the sea and an attack could come from

Back on board is usually a very happy time. The first order is the customary informal conference, each one relating his adventures. Here we are seeking some shade from the heat of the sun and perhaps a little cooling breeze.

any direction. In addition to this, proximity to the surface seems to excite sharks and makes the actual moment of leaving the water dangerous.

The squaloscope was empty. The two captured sharks had twisted the light aluminum bars out of shape at their centers and succeeded in escaping. Even twisted in this fashion, the spacing between the bars was inconsiderable and it must have been necessary for the sharks to pass through them on their sides; I marveled at the strength that made this possible. Bernard Mestre, who was accompanying Canoë, made a ligature joining together all the bars at their center and thus reinforcing the squaloscope. This time we did not use any hook; the morsels of fish were simply tied to the rope held by Canoë. In this way, we hoped to prevent any captured sharks from demolishing the squaloscope, as the one he had hooked that morning had almost done. Bernard Chauvellin, who was my bodyguard, stayed close behind me, ready to protect me from the rear and to assist either of the two others.

There were more sharks than there had been in the morning, but the *ambiance* was even more mistrustful. I speak of ambiance because, to an experienced diver, there is a different ambiance connected with every dive. And with sharks, ambiance is of fundamental importance. Sometimes we sense that we can caress them or ignore them, and at other times we are immediately conscious of danger. I have known dives in which, although the sharks showed no change of attitude and continued circling at the same speed, we all felt and shared a spontaneous nervousness. At such times we become wary, ready for action. The warning is never ignored, even though it may be vague and inexplicable. And at other times, although nothing may have changed in appearance, we sense that we are secure and know instinctively that we can approach the animals with impunity.

Thirty or so of the "black fins" — the reef sharks — and ten to fifteen of the *Albimarginatus* with the white-bordered fins were circling slowly around the squaloscope. A small grouper had now made it his residence and remained undisturbed as we went about our work on the sand floor surrounding his improvised shelter. This time, our operations had been meticulously programed in advance and we were able to carry them out more efficiently. In a short space of time, four of the black-finned sharks were captured and we began our experiments. We planned to try out several different anesthetics, with the object of tranquillizing the sharks and thereby permitting us to carry out further research. Among other things, we hoped to be able to cover their eyes, both to test their sense of smell and to facilitate the placement of electrodes for an encephalogram.

To begin with, we tried out a whitish liquid known as product MS-222, which is well known to biologists, who use it in the capture of live specimens of fish. We administered it to the sharks through a giant syringe whose piston or plunger is operated by a compressed-air cyclinder. Since the pressure of air contained in the cylinder is greater than that of the surrounding pressure, the product is expelled in a great cloud of white liquid when a valve is opened.

Bernard Mestre caught hold of a pectoral fin on one of our captive sharks and pulled the animal up against the bars of the squaloscope. Despite his frenzied struggling, Canoë plunged the tube of the syringe into the shark's mouth and released the valve. The syringe emptied itself and the water grew cloudy everywhere around the shark's head, in front of his mouth as well as behind his gills. When the syringe was entirely empty, Bernard released him, and the animal immediately resumed his circling within the squaloscope, ramming his snout against its sides, just as he had been doing before. We waited in vain for some sign of weakening, but he seemed absolutely impervious to the product and went on swimming, with no sign of tiring.

We have tried all kinds of products and methods, with varying but seldom satisfactory results. As a last resort, we considered a highly French technique: the injection of cognac. Doctor Eugenie Clark had advised us to try hypodermic shots of alcohol, but since we had no alcohol on board and the concentration of it in cognac was sufficient, we decided to use it as a substitute. I remember Doctor François standing on the afterdeck, with his graduated receptacles and his big veterinary's syringe, waiting for my father, who came on deck carrying an unopened bottle of three-star cognac. Obviously, before the syringe could be filled, the cognac had to be tested and that could not be done without obtaining the opinion of all the divers. At last, however, the syringe was full and we went down the diving ladder. It was a joyful experiment, and everyone seemed hopeful that it would succeed. The level of cognac remaining in the bottle bore witness to the numerous trial runs we had thought necessary before applying the theories of scientific authority. This time, the ambiance of the dive was one of pronounced optimism. Unfortunately, when we reached the bottom, we found only dead sharks in the squaloscope. Our subconscious awareness of a serious situation returned at once. The waters around us were deserted, and of all the sharks

A typical aspect of the shark in open sea with the sun playing through the surface on his back.

that had been here earlier, only the four motionless forms in the squaloscope remained.

Canoë set down the now-useless syringe and reached through the bars of the cage to catch hold of the tail of one of the sharks. He was indeed dead, and so were all three of the others. Far off, at the very limit of our vision, I could make out several slowly circling forms. They were sharks, but they had suddenly become cautious and remained at a considerable distance from us. The cognac was forgotten as we tried in vain to coax these vague and faraway silhouettes to return. Our pieces of fresh fish attracted only the little grouper, and it was not until after we had removed the dead sharks that we were able to continue with our experiments. What could it have been that caused this signal of mistrust to carry across the water?

Other experiments, carried out in Florida and in the Pacific, have shown that the odor of dead sharks effectively repels other squali. One of my father's close friends, Conrad Limbaugh (who has since been the victim of a diving accident while visiting an undersea cavern), has described one of these experiments. While he was with a group of ichthyologists studying the shark populations surrounding Clipperton Island in the Pacific, several dead sharks were left on the beach one day. Two days later, their carcasses, which had been cut open for dissection, began to rot and the liquids produced by decomposition ran down the sloping sands in long rust-colored rivulets. Shortly thereafter, the sharks, which had been extremely abundant in these waters, abandoned the area completely.

Intrigued by this fact, our friend then carried out systematic experiments with meat in varying stages of decomposition, using it as bait on his lines. Sharks did not even approach it. These interesting results did not, however, lead to more extensive experimentation, for a very simple reason. The system, however effective it might have been, had disastrous effects on the experimenters, since the smell of the putrid meat caused violent attacks of seasickness.

Among the professional shark fishermen of South Africa or Florida, it is a well-known fact that it is useless to leave a sharkline in the water for more than a few days. These men use as many as two hundred hooks to a line, and they know that sharks caught on the first day will die within a few hours. After the third day, no living shark will approach the bait.

On board the *Calypso,* we verified this fact many times: if a dead shark was left on the bottom, the others disappeared within a matters of hours.

It is possible that a more detailed study of these facts would lead to the discovery of an effective product for repelling sharks and protecting swimmers. Since Mr. Limbaugh utilized not only shark meat but also the meat of other fish, the widespread belief that squali eat only spoiled flesh was proven false. In cases of extreme famine, some sharks may accept a bait of putrid meat, but such cases are rare.

Our sharks in the squaloscope were dead simply because it was too small. They had died of asphyxiation. The majority of sharks, such as the great white shark *(Carcharodon carcharias),* the blue shark *(Isurus glaucus),* the black-finned reef shark *(Carcharhinus maculipinnis),* and the hammerhead *(Sphyrna lewini),* among many other species, swim unceasingly, day and night. There are two reasons for this, one being that sharks do not possess a "swimming bladder" — that organ which can be inflated at will and permits fish to stabilize themselves at different depths; if sharks stop swimming they will sink. The other reason for this continuous movement is the fact that sharks, with the exception of some species, have no mechanism for pumping water so that it will pass over their gills and the oxygen will be transferred to the blood stream. In other species of fish, the mouth is constantly in action, to create a continuous current of water over the gills, even in the absence of any actual movement on the part of the fish. The common goldfish, for example, can remain perfectly still in his glass tank and breathe easily. The majority of sharks, however, depend for their respiration on their movement through the water. Our squaloscope was too confined in its dimensions and condemned the sharks it contained to asphyxiation, because it prevented them from swimming continuously and fast enough.

Since our own experience with the death of the sharks, Doctor Clark has given us several other examples of the same problem. Sharks on which experiments have been carried out can be revived by forcing them to swim in their tanks; divers push or pull them through the water until they have regained consciousness. And in a reverse example of the same situation, sharks employed for the filming of such adventure spectacles as *Thunderball* were tranquillized by being towed backward or simply immobilized for a certain period of time.

We have adopted other, more effective methods of capture, but I shall always remember that big metal-and-plastic structure resting on the sands of Abu Marina. The reef sharks that surrounded it taught us a valuable lesson. At a time when we were becoming too sure of ourselves and relaxing our security provisions, they showed us to what extent nature and the sea are perverse and changeable. That precarious return to the surface was a warning that went home to each of us and reinforced the security precautions of the whole team.

The sum total of these experiments was, however, far from being negative. In addition to valuable information on the behavior of sharks, we had arrived at a more complete understanding of the techniques to be used in the study of sharks in captivity. But such a study, in an enclosed area, presented logistical problems of transportation and preparation. Therefore, it seemed clear that the next phase of our operations should be directed toward the study of sharks at liberty.

SIX:

Bullfight in the Deep
We tag sharks with darts.
The nine-foot *longimanus.*
Territorial claims of sharks.

Philippe Cousteau's narrative continues

My camera is pointed toward Raymond Coll, who has just left the big steel cage and is swimming slowly, holding his spear ready for use. From the corner of my eye I can see a blue shark more than nine feet long, moving on a course that will converge with Raymond's. The shark seems indifferent to the diver, who is now describing a gentle curve that brings him closer to the animal with every movement of his arms or his rubber fins. As he approaches the point of contact, Raymond accelerates slightly, stepping up the rhythm of his swimming just a trifle. The shark's round eye does not leave him for a second. They are now less than six feet apart, and still approaching each other. I release the shutter of the camera, and its clicking sound seems to act as a signal. Raymond's arm reaches out and the tip of the spear penetrates the flesh at the base of the dorsal fin. With a single flick of his enormous tail, the blue shark streaks off to a distance of about sixty feet and then resumes his lazy course. The turbulence he has caused in the water has almost upended the diver, who is now prudently retreating to the cage, followed by two gray sharks with white fins. Raymond glances at me and lifts a thumb in triumph. His normally impassive eyes are glittering behind his mask; he has succeeded.

I turn back toward the shark and can see that, although still some distance away, he is coming back toward us, but slowly and apparently indifferent to us. When he passes in front of me, I can make out the swirling movement of the little yellow plaque attached to the short banderilla Raymond has just planted beside his dorsal fin. This is the fourteenth animal we have

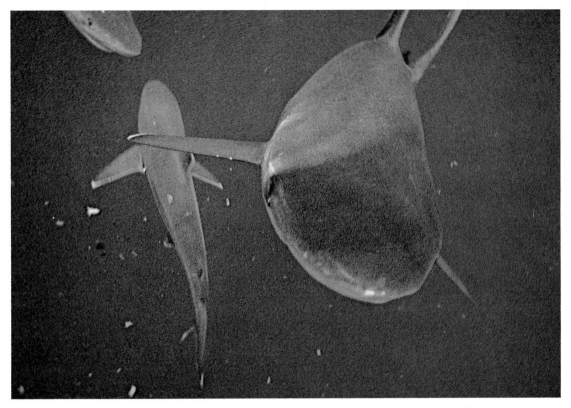

He is coming straight at the camera. Those small white dots that can be seen are crumbs of fish, which are not enough of a mouthful for the shark. They are not even bite-size, but the smell they generate in the water excites the sharks immensely. These sharks are called *Albimarginatus,* the white-tip reef sharks found in the Red Sea.

marked today, and he will also be the last. I give the signal for return to the surface and the ship.

This is a much less simple sport than it might appear to be. Not all sharks are as good subjects as the big *Galeocerdo cuvieri;* most of them react more rapidly and their reactions are dangerous. To "mark" an animal, Raymond must approach to within less than four feet of him, then plant the point of the spear as close as possible to the dorsal fin and quickly withdraw the shaft. This leaves a banderilla of treated stainless steel planted in a region in which the shark's flesh is most firm and where it will in no way irritate him. Attached to the banderilla by a thread of plaited nylon is a plaquette of orange plastic, bearing a number and the address of the Oceanographic Museum of Monaco.

On two separate occasions today, a shark has turned back on our im-

The shark cage in action. Two movie lights are attached to the upper side of the cage, while one diver is pointing to a shark, ready to set out to tag him. In his left hand he is holding a spear, which will serve as a tagging device.

promptu matador, jaws wickedly open, and Raymond has had to beat a quick retreat to the cage. Fortunately, the animals had not pressed their attack, and after a time they had gone away. I have been watching this undersea *corrida* with a feeling of unreality bordering on the miraculous. Even the bright colors are there, the yellow-gold, the red, and the royal blue, while the trumpet and trombone sounds from our regulators and our air bubbles provide music for the *fiesta brava*. All the divers wanted to try their hands at this new sport, but it is unquestionably Raymond Coll who has had the greatest success at it — perhaps because of his Spanish ancestry. Nonetheless, I am still a trifle uneasy about it. This is not a single bull that he must face, but an entire herd, with a whole realm of space in which to retreat and attack again. It is a three-dimensional *corrida* which has been taking place before my eyes.

We began this experiment with the goal of studying the mode of life of the Red Sea sharks. My father had noticed that, quite often, one reef might have a considerable population of sharks while the adjoining reef, just a few miles away, had none. Moreover, because it was often possible to recognize sharks by their distinctive scars (almost all of them bore scars), it seemed that the same population of sharks always frequented the same corner of the sea Very little is known about the migrations of sharks; at the very most we do know that, at certain times of the year, large gatherings of some species have been seen in areas of shallow water or in the estuaries of large rivers. Numerous research centers throughout the world, notably in South Africa and Australia, are devoting themselves to the study of the possibility of large-scale shark migrations. To this day, however, no real light has been shed on the subject; we do not even know if sharks do, in fact, migrate from one region to another. The problem of a suitable material for marking the animals is certainly one of the most important restraining factors in such a study. The majority of marking devices are rejected in a relatively short period by the shark's organic system. This was the case with ours; but they may also be bitten or torn off by another animal or scraped off by contact with rocks or sunken wrecks.

Our program was less ambitious than any such detailed study. We wanted simply to learn whether the shark known as a "reef shark" was a sedentary animal or moved from one reef to another in search of food. And we knew that the plaquettes we used for marking would probably remain in place no more than a few months. Another of our goals was to establish whether, in the event that the sharks are sedentary, they maintain a territory exclusive

The diver is going out now. Having shifted his spear to the right hand, he is diving straight toward the shark.

Now he is letting the shark go by and will swim as quickly as possible to place himself along the shark's side.

With cameraman Michel Deloire in the right-hand corner, the diver, Raymond Coll, is swimming straight for the shark. Not unlike a bullfighter handling his *banderillas,* the diver must anticipate all movements of the shark and react accordingly.

to themselves, as do a great many reef- or shore-living species. Obviously, if the sharks turned out to be sedentary, any further experiments we might attempt would be facilitated, since they would learn to accept our presence among them.

In the course of a week we marked more than one hundred and ten sharks in the vicinity of eight reefs or islets of the Suakin group, in the Red Sea. Aside from the great blue shark of that first day, we had encountered only some *Albimarginatus* and a few of the *Carcharhinus obscurus* which inhabit these coral reefs. Then we left the region for three weeks, to carry out some other work in the south and outside of Djibouti.

On Friday the twenty-ninth of September, the day after our return, Paul Zuéna tossed into the water a two-pound bait of meat, along with the large hook on which it hung. I was in the water, and Paul's movements, deformed by the refracted light from the surface just above me, seemed somehow monstrous. As he manipulated his line, his silhouette danced against a background of blue sky, resembling a pygmy with gigantic arms sowing seed across the waters. The shark climbed straight from the depths, emerging from the shadows on an absolutely vertical course toward the bait, which now floated at the center of a circle of concentric ripplings. He resembled nothing so much as a projectile perfectly adjusted on its target. Again, it was a large *Albimarginatus,* about seven or eight feet long, but his rounded belly bore witness to recent feeding and, in fact, he hesitated for a long time before biting. After he had circled for a quarter of an hour, some other sharks entered into the circle and showed signs of attacking the bait. This was all that was needed. One last time, the big shark turned in front of my cage, clearly displaying the yellow plaque at the base of his dorsal fin, and then swallowed the hook.

A shark's manner of eating is extraordinarily supple. He neither speeds toward the prey nor does he slow down; he seems simply to breathe in the portion he has chosen, which disappears into his still-opened mouth as he passes on. But should that portion contain a hook, the mouth and the entire body is seized with a violent convulsion as it penetrates the flesh, and he hurls himself forward with all his strength, thus pushing the hook further into his flesh.

I could guess that Paul would be watching his line as it streaked out, accompanied by the shrill whistling of his carefully soaped reel. Encountering no resistance, the shark slowed down and Paul took the line in hand, beginning to draw it in, slowly, gently, but ceaselessly. Now the shark began to fight back furiously, beating against the surface of the water with his tail, or plunging desperately toward the bottom. The others, watching him, had drawn back a little but were still not far away. One of them, in fact, had swallowed the portion of meat our captive had coughed up in his efforts to regurgitate the hook. Now, they were circling like vultures, ready to profit from anything that might develop. The captive shark lost strength very quickly and his defensive actions became weaker — this brute of an animal was a fragile prey. For one thing, the line on which he was hooked immobilized him, hindering the continuous flow of water through his gills, and thus asphyxiating him; and for another, his internal constitution also contributed to this weakness. There is no sustaining ligament, no muscle to hold a shark's intestines in place; the natural intestinal support is the water outside the fine abdominal wall. As soon as a shark is taken from the water and no longer has this support beneath his abdomen, his thin skin distends and his internal organs are torn apart by the effect of weight. Once removed from the water, even if he is immediately returned to it and swims off quite normally, a shark is almost certainly condemned to death, since the chaos created in his intestines will no longer permit them to function normally. But even if his struggle for life is short — and this is not true of all species — the shark does not die easily.

When I returned to the deck of the *Calypso,* I watched, with no joy in my heart, as our old enemy died. All his beauty had vanished; he lay there, limp, dirty, pathetic, his scarred and tortured tail beating the rhythm of a final swim. This sort of thing may go on for an hour or more with a dying shark, and many men have suffered a nasty wound because they imprudently ventured too close to the animal. The great mouth of our shark still snapped at the void and his soiled body quivered and trembled for a long time. Canoë removed the marking plaque and went off with it to my father's cabin. After a final glance at the expiring shark, I followed him. When we consulted our marking records — the books which told us where and on what date each shark had been marked — we found that this particular animal had been marked in exactly this same place a month before.

Of some sixty-five recovered plaques, the same result occurred in fifty-seven cases. The species of shark we had marked was obviously sedentary, at least during a part of the year. This observation, however, was extremely inconclusive, since there was nothing to inform us of the habits of these same sharks at other times of the year. The laboratories or scientific institutions

The diver is now in position and has raised his arm, to plant the small tag in the shark's skin.

There you see the spear being withdrawn, in the upper left-hand corner, and leaving the little tag on the shark's back on the right of the dorsal fin.

There it is. The shark is marked, and the diver accompanies him for a few seconds.
(Note: Vertical lines are scratches in the original motion picture negative.)

that concentrate on this matter have set up systematic specifications for marking. But the difficulties in such a process are enormous and we had neither the time nor the means to overcome them.

Shortly after we had established the first principle of the sedentary character of these sharks, we recognized a second — territoriality. When it is said that a shark possesses a territory, it would seem to indicate that a portion of the reef is reserved to him. Every day, when we dived in the same spot, we saw the same sharks, recognizing them most often by their scars. This is not, however, an absolute rule, since the same shark may be seen elsewhere on the reef, while other sharks are patrolling his territory. They are tolerated there; the possession of a territory does not mean that the shark expels all others from it. He contents himself with the knowledge that he is master of it. We have verified this same principle with many other species of fish — groupers, trigger fish, some varieties of lion fish, moray eels. A large shark will admit other sharks to his territory, on condition that they do not pose a problem of direct competition. They are reduced to seeking their food on a catch-as-catch-can basis, far from the eyes of the master, and they eat in his presence only when he leaves them the remains or when his prey is so large that he is occupied with eating on one side and cannot immediately attend to them. If these rules are not respected, there is instant warfare, testified to by the scars left on one shark's skin by the bite of another. But even these rules, which may be set for one corner of a reef, are often upset by the appearance of a foreign and stronger animal. Like a duke descending on some petty baron, the great ocean shark occasionally descends on his less hardy or more fearful vassals.

Shortly after our second stay on the Suakin reefs, we returned to the reef surrounding Dahl Ghab Island (near the western edge of the Red Sea, off Sudan), to continue with our marking program. At the same time, we inaugurated a communications system which permitted me to speak directly by telephone to my father or to anyone else on the bridge of the *Calypso*.

In the larger cage, Marcel Soudre was in charge of the long marking spear and drew sharks toward him by throwing out a morsel of fish from time to time. I was in a smaller, individual cage, facing Marcel's, with my camera ready to film. Fifteen or so sharks of two separate species were circling around us. There were several large *Albimarginatus,* and the others were very supple gray sharks. I recognized the lord of the manor immediately; he was an old *Albimarginatus* whose mouth had been torn apart at one side, leaving a scarred and gaping hole when it healed. He was swimming peacefully, and it was perfectly clear that the others were avoiding him. He was a frequent visitor in these parts, almost an old friend. He had come to watch us in every one of our dives in this spot. We had marked him several days before, and he had turned on us, seeking to bite. He gave us the impression of a tough old warrior, wary and precise. Whenever another shark sped toward a piece of our fish, he struck at him as hard and swift as a missile, and the other abandoned his prey. It sometimes happened, however, that the smaller shark was able to eat and get away before he was caught, and in this case the big *Albimarginatus* ceased his pursuit and resumed his circling, wasting no time on useless anger.

It was in this atmosphere of well-established order that we set out to mark the last sharks of the group. I had exhausted the magazine of one camera, so I telephoned to the surface and asked that another be sent down. When it arrived, loaded with four hundred feet of new film, I was preparing to adjust the F-stop and focus when I glimpsed a dark mass just at the limits of my vision — about a hundred and fifty feet away. Then I began to notice that the sharks, which had been coming up to us more and more readily for the past half hour, were now nervous and wary. At first, I did not understand what had happened, since I did not associate the vague form I had seen with this new attitude of the sharks surrounding me. This situation went on for several minutes, and then, at last, I understood everything. The cause of the sudden agitation was approaching.

I recognized it as one of the most formidable of the deep-sea sharks, a great *longimanus,* well known to my father and all of us, more than nine feet in length and accompanied by at least eighteen pilot fish, each of them a good-sized animal. It was because of this moving cloud that I had not at first recognized the shark in the somewhat cloudy water.

While the brute strength of other sharks is tempered by their beauty and the elegance of their form and movement, this species is absolutely hideous. His yellow-brown color is not uniform, but streaked with irregular markings resembling a bad job of military camouflage. His body is rounder than that of other sharks and the extremities of his enormous pectoral fins and his rounded dorsal fin look as if they had been dyed a dirty gray. He swims in a jerky, irregular manner, swinging his shortened, broad snout from side to side. His tiny eyes are hard and cruel-looking. The cloud of pilot fish changes shape, sometimes scattering and then drawing closer together in an uncertain, nervous rhythm. From time to time, one fish will detach itself from the group and go off to inspect an object of some kind, then hastily return and take up its former place. Two large remoras and one smaller one form dark spots on the shark's belly.

I had a vague consciousness of sudden silence, and when I became more fully aware of it I realized that I myself had been breathing more slowly, almost as though I was attempting to hide. A few feet in front of me, Marcel too had forgotten his work and was watching the intruder. The big white-finned shark had disappeared, and the others were swimming rapidly, furtively, keeping well away from the newcomer. Sharks accompanied by pilot fish have already been compared with great Flying Fortresses surrounded by a squadron of fighter planes, and it is an image which gives a clear impression of the destructive force embodied in this vision.

This particular shark was swimming in lazy circles, about fifty feet from

The shark is gulping the lure, a piece of fish meat which we put on the hook of Paul's line. After a period of time, we fished the sharks to withdraw the tags, in order to learn of their migrating habits. This one is a white-tip shark about eight feet long.

The shark has swallowed the whole lure and is about to be hooked.

He is now pulling at the line. We can barely discern the red tag he is wearing just behind the dorsal fin. He is a good catch.

The shark is pulled out and the tag will be removed, to be logged in the book for subsequent study.

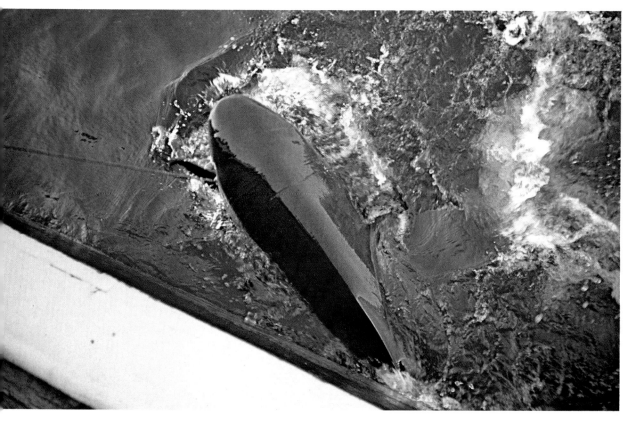

our cages, but his mere presence had brought the scent of fear to this little corner of the ocean. A few more minutes passed, and then I reacted at last. I was not going to permit this animal to ruin our dive, so I signaled to Marcel to go on with his work. A morsel of fish was waved about outside the cage, and when a small shark darted forward to seize it, Marcel managed to mark him perfectly. While I was checking my camera to see how much film remained, I saw the *longimanus* again. He seemed to be paying no attention to us and had even moved a trifle farther away. Marcel had no more fish with which to attract the other sharks within range of his spear, so I used up the rest of my film on random shots of the sharks remaining in the area. I was on the point of signaling for us to be brought to the surface when I was suddenly surrounded by a rustling flight of black-and-white pilot fish. They had left the shark, as if at some mysterious signal, and were circling about me like a swarm of moths around a flame. About fifty feet from my cage, the great ocean shark turned suddenly and hurled himself forward at incredible speed. In a fraction of a second he was beneath the stern of the *Calypso* and had snatched at the gleaming casing of the transmitter-receiver of the undersea telephone, which was hanging just below the surface. The cable was sliced in two as cleanly as if by a giant pair of scissors. The shark turned violently back on himself and furiously coughed up the metal box, which promptly sank to the bottom. Without a moment's pause, the shark arrowed his huge body toward Marcel, who had just time enough to close the door of his cage. The shark ricocheted away like a bullet, and turned straight toward me, seizing the bars of the cage in his jaw — a scant six inches from my face — and shaking it like a madman. I had a vision of the rope to the surface being cut and the cage drifting down, leaving me no alternative but to try and get back to the ship on my own, exposing myself to this frenzied attack. And then, abandoning the twisted bars of the cage, he turned again and disappeared as swiftly as he had attacked, followed by his straining escort of pilot fish.

It seemed to me that I remained there for an eternity, motionless, almost without breathing. I had not had time to be afraid before. Marcel was watching me, and I was dimly aware of a great plume of air bubbles around his head. At last, I could feel the cage going up, and I emerged in the blinding sunlight. I climbed out of the cage, feeling curiously calm and preoccupied with insignificant things like the seam of my diving suit or the position of a length of rope. My father's appearance brought me back to reality. He had

This is the great *longimanus* during daytime. He is accompanied by one pilot fish, in the foreground, and several more above him, swimming just below the surface. His gray-brown markings are quite irregular, and he has more of a dirty appearance than the painted look of other sharks. His extremely wide fins provide him with good control over his movements in water. Pilot fish do not steer the shark. They merely accompany him for the leftovers from his meals.

Emerging from a long dive is a good moment, as the sun hits your face and warms your skin; and you know you have some good material inside the camera.

seen everything on the undersea television screen which watches all our operations, and his laughter was a little more hearty than usual. . . .

Later that day I made another dive under the same working conditions. The great ocean shark did not show himself this time, and I thought of him with a kind of secret jealousy. This solitary hunter — a minuscule but formidable figure in the immensity of the sea — had returned to his own domain. The other sharks seemed smaller to me now, reduced to their own petty quarrels, to their own little hierarchy. The old *Albimarginatus* had reappeared, but far from being the lord of the manor, he now seemed nothing more than a country squire, marked with our plaque as dutifully as a domestic animal wearing a license.

In the course of all our studies of sharks, we have often verified this idea of distinct territories. Not only have we determined the existence of local hierarchies, by which a shark who is master of the southern area of a reef may be just tolerated in the north, where another is the ruler, but we have also verified the fact that few or no sharks change territories. Intrigued by stories of shark fisheries that have selected a particular location because of the abundance of its shark population, and then gone bankrupt two or three years later, we decided to try the same system. We spent two days fishing for sharks near the island of Gharb Myun in the Farasan Islands. At the end of this period, the only sharks remaining in the area were some small *Albimarginatus,* measuring no more than three or four feet. Thanks to Paul Zuéna's skill as a fisherman, we had caught all the larger sharks of that territory. The tiny island surrounded by the reef of Gharb Myun is located at a distance of only one or two miles from the other reefs and islands of the group. And yet, in all of our dives there, we encountered only those sharks we had spared and marked during our previous stay. This does not mean that the reef had not been visited by other sharks; it certainly had been, but they had probably returned to their own territories. We feel quite sure that the small sharks of this region will grow rapidly and take complete possession of it, now that our fishing experiments have provided them with a more abundant source of nourishment and less competition.

In the course of these active weeks, we had tried to pierce the mystery surrounding the daily lives of the squali of this area, and our knowledge had greatly increased. But now, prodded on by the passage of time, we abandoned this study and set out to shed some light on another aspect of the existence of sharks — their reactions when faced with man.

SEVEN:
Arthur's Experience with the *Albimarginatus*
Arthur's frightful ordeal.
The feeding habits of sharks.
Best means of protection.
Experiments with antishark products.

Philippe Cousteau's narrative continues

Today, I was diving with Arthur, to study the behavior of sharks when confronted with an undefended diver. A few sharks, their fins and tail bordered with white, could be seen swimming in the clear water surrounding the *Calypso*. They seemed lazy, even indolent, almost as though they were attempting to conceal their strength behind the façade of a peaceful appearance. I went down the ladder first and swam immediately to the antishark cage suspended about thirty feet beneath the keel of the ship. The *Calypso* was anchored about one hundred feet off the reef of Dahl Ghab, in the southwest portion of the Red Sea; the water below the keel was approximately five hundred feet in depth. It was a day of torrid heat, without a breath of wind, and I was far more comfortable in the water than I had felt on deck. A few feet away, Arthur had just entered the water and was beginning his somewhat awkward evolutions back and forth in front of the cage. Although the only result of my entrance into the water had been to focus the attention of the few sharks in the immediate vicinity, Arthur's more clumsy arrival had attracted other animals and their lazy swimming had abruptly become rapid.

I kept my camera pointed toward Arthur, whose face mask was now reflecting the sunlight in blinding rays. What a perfect prey he was, completely without defense. His jerky movements could doubtless be heard at a considerable distance by the sensitive hearing system of the shark, and the rays of the sun glittering from his mask constituted a virtual call to murder. The atmosphere had changed almost at once; the slightly obscene swaying motion of sharks when they are swimming without any definite goal had given way to the supple, precise movements of the animal in a state of alert. There were

The great shark coming at the diver is an *Albimarginatus,* a white-tip reef shark. The "diver" here is fortunately a dummy we used to test the reaction of sharks to the fully dressed diver. The shark circled for a fairly long time, the usual period. It was a huge shark, probably well fed, judging from the roundness of his belly. Hunger was not a driving force in him. He tore one leg off the dummy, which we dubbed Arthur, and came back for more. At that point we knew enough and pulled the dummy out. This experiment proved that whether or not a diver is covered by a layer of foam rubber, he is vulnerable to sharks.

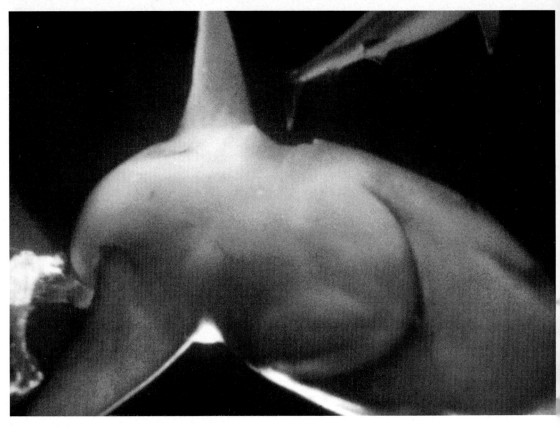

The shark confronts the camera before disappearing in the dark.

now seven or eight sharks swimming around us. I recognized two large *Albimarginatus,* more than six feet in length, among some very slender gray sharks with extremely small pectoral fins, but I was unable to identify these. Suddenly, something in their attitude changed, and I noticed at once that they were now swimming abreast of each other, straight toward us. One of the big *Albimarginatus* swerved, very rapidly, and swept up toward Arthur. At the last moment, he turned away and sped off into the distance, followed by all the others. It was several seconds before I realized that my camera was still running. I had been so startled by the suddenness of the attack that I had forgotten I was holding it. Arthur was still moving impassively in the sun, just above and in front of me. Off in the distance, the big shark turned gracefully in the water and came back, straight toward us again. This time, he seemed to be aiming for Arthur's back, but his mouth brushed against the right leg instead. He turned again, his mouth open, and I could hear across the water the terrible sound of the monster's teeth closing on — steel. The shark shook

his head furiously and tore off the dummy's leg, leaving only the steel armature sticking out of the rubber diving suit like a broken tibia.

I shut off my camera and returned quickly to the cage, since all the
sharks were now hurling themselves indiscriminately at anything in the water.
One of them smashed against the cage, and then darted off in the direction of
Arthur, who was being hauled out of the water by the men on the deck above
us. I signaled for my cage to be brought up too. After what I had just seen,
I felt reluctant to leave it and swim the short distance to the diving ladder.

When I set foot on the deck, the faces around me were grave. My companions were standing in a little group surrounding the mutilated form of the
dummy lying on the stretcher we had used for carrying it. I knew what they
were thinking. Each one of them was imagining a face behind the empty mask,
his own, perhaps, or that of any one of us. I tried to shake off the macabre
atmosphere by suggesting, in a somewhat nervous voice, that what remained
of the dummy should be thrown back in the water. But my remark had no
effect on the general gloom of the scene; I had come close to using the word
"corpse" in speaking of the dummy, and throwing it back in the water would
have had too much resemblance to the burial of a sailor at sea. Someone
jokingly suggested that we might read a prayer for Arthur, but the pleasantry
was met with glacial silence. All through the rest of the day we were moody
and morose, and my sleep that night was peopled with frightful visions. For
several weeks after that, everyone redoubled his security measures and dis-
played new respect for any sharks we encountered.

The idea behind the construction of Arthur was to discover whether the
rubber diving suit and the aspect of a diver under water were sufficient to
drive off sharks. It had, in fact, been our settled belief in the past that attacks
on fully suited and equipped scuba divers by sharks had never had tragic
consequences. We had, therefore, fabricated Arthur from an armature of steel
bars, dressed him in one of Yves Omer's diving suits, and stuffed him with
foam rubber. A small, round watermelon was placed in a helmet to represent
the head, and a plastic facsimile of one of our aqualungs completed the silhouette. Outwardly, Arthur was an exact duplicate of our own appearance
undersea.

The first experiments we carried out with him had had no results. We
were not particularly surprised by this, since it would have been rather strange
if an object of steel, plastic, and rubber had attracted the interest of an eater
of meat and fish. We performed these experiments only when the sharks were

The great *longimanus* surrounded by his court, or cloud of pilot fish, is interested in the dead carcass in the foreground. The *Carcharhinus longimanus* is certainly one of the most dangerous species. Individuals are only found in high seas and very seldom come close to shore, but they are very determined. They will attack in spite of all the means of defense we employ, and they will not get discouraged as would many other species of shark. They are ugly but also quite powerful.

It is the same shark, the *longimanus,* bearing our tag on the left side of his dorsal fin. The *longimanus* is fairly squat and his fins are not pointed; they are rounded at the edge. His head is large and round. His color here appears to be metallic gray, but it is more on the brown side during daylight. This one has a bellyful of food and is not so aggressive any more.

This is his head, mouth opened. The teeth are not clearly visible because they are embedded in the flesh of his mouth. They become erect only when the shark is taking a bite. His eye, as you can see, looks cruel and cold.

calm, since we knew that if we tossed Arthur into the water in the midst of one of their frenzies, he would immediately be torn apart, as would any other object in the water at such a moment. The experiment could not, however, be considered perfect because of the impossibility of giving life to the dummy; and no one will contest the fact that animals, even sharks, know the difference between the quick and the dead. We decided, therefore, to provide Arthur with an enticing scent.

To accomplish this, we had tried all kinds of products, from beef bouillon, in which we had soaked the foam rubber that padded the steel frame of the dummy, to bits of fish hidden in the diving suit itself. We had just seen the results obtained from the experiment with bits of fresh fish inserted in the dummy. We had, however, noticed that the attack was not nearly so immediate as it would have been had the same portions of fish been thrown directly into the sea. We think the rubber suit is a form of protection that is not to be

This picture shows the size of one bite by a shark of eight or nine feet—average length. The bites are round and clean-cut, due to the sawing lateral movement of the head and the shape of the teeth, with their sharp, serrated edges.

neglected, even though it is in no sense sufficient. Moreover, it is possible that the scent of the human body is not particularly enticing to sharks. And lastly, there is also the possibility that our shape and size, as well as the color of our diving suits, cause us to bear some resemblance to dolphins — and the shark never attacks a dolphin unless he knows him to be injured, weakened by illness, or in some other way disabled.

One of the many widespread legends on the subject of sharks, and one of the hardest to dispel, is to the effect that the shark is a carrion-eater and appreciates more than anything else meat that is spoiled or in the process of decomposition. There are no facts whatever to support this theory. I think that a famished shark will bite into anything at all: according to the extent of his hunger, this might be a wooden plank or a corpse in decomposition, but neither the former — obviously — nor the latter forms part of his preferred diet. I have seen sharks bite into hooks baited with beef, but their movements have always been lacking in real desire, and when they did eventually bite, it was only after a long period of hesitation. I remember that, during an earlier cruise, we had been obliged to rid ourselves of an entire side of beef because a breakdown in the cold-storage system had made our supply of meat unfit for consumption. The enormous package had been wrapped in sackcloth, heavily ballasted, and sunk on a corner of sand just at the edge of the coral shelf of the reef where we were anchored. For several days thereafter, the side of beef remained intact, even though there were many sharks in the area. It was not until after a week had passed that the meat disappeared, and when a tiger shark, which we had noticed in the preceding days because of his size and his lean and hungry look, appeared with swollen and distended abdomen, we realized what had happened. The shark's lack of enthusiasm for this particular prey had been conquered by his hunger. We were also struck by the fact that a shark only about ten feet in length could have swallowed an entire side of beef.

To be sure, deep-sea sharks follow schools of mammals, and sometimes follow ships, to feed from their leavings, but this means nothing in itself, since these castoffs are always fresh food. Moreover, it is our belief that the energy requirements of sharks are very small; they are inclined to swim in open, unobstructed waters in which the slightest movement on their part propels them over a considerable distance. They do not suffer from cold, and their calorie loss must be minimal, so that one good meal should permit them to exist for a very long time.

Here he is passing behind the cage to get to the food. With open mouth, he closes in for the attack very, very rapidly.

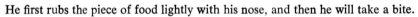

He first rubs the piece of food lightly with his nose, and then he will take a bite.

Here you can see the pilot fish under his belly coming in with him to eat the crumbs.

Mouth open, he goes in for a twenty-pound mouthful.

The study of the shark's digestive system provides some support for this theory. Shark's intestines, as compared with those of mammals, are extremely short: an adult man has intestines approximately thirty feet in length, while a nine-foot shark has a maximum of about seven feet. Moreover, sharks seem to have the incredible ability to digest only certain portions of their stomach contents, while other portions remain almost intact for long periods. This may be a form of natural reserve which permits the sharks to live for some time by storing and preserving a single meal. Sir Edward Allstrom, director of the Taranga Zoo, near Sydney, Australia, has recounted the case of a fifteen-foot tiger shark housed in one of the zoo's tanks. Over a period of twenty-one days, the shark rejected the horse meat it was fed, first swallowing it and then vomiting it a few days later. The shark died, and an examination of the contents of his stomach revealed two perfectly preserved dolphins. They had probably been devoured a few hours before the capture of the shark. But how he had been able to preserve the dolphins intact while rejecting other food remains an enigma.

It is in this same zoo that studies have been made on the quantity of nourishment absorbed by sharks. In his book, *Shark Attack,* V. M. Coppleson cites the cases of two sharks, one of them eleven and a half feet in length, the other just about ten feet, and each weighing approximately three hundred and fifty pounds. In one year, the first shark consumed one hundred and ninety pounds of fish, while the other consumed two hundred and twenty. He also noted a very sharp decline in the sharks' food requirements during the winter months — from May to August, in Australia. It would seem, therefore, that the nutritional needs of sharks are well below those of insatiable voracity, for which they have acquired a reputation.

Over the years, we aboard *Calypso* have been impressed by the briefness of elapsed time in a shark frenzy, even more than by its violence, however incredible that may be. During one night dive, I saw four sharks attack a wounded dolphin and tear him to bits, within a matter of minutes, despite all our feeble efforts with spears and shark billies. Nothing could have resisted these demons incarnate. They bit into the dolphin's flesh, tearing away a mouthful of anything from sixteen to twenty pounds, then turned back and bit again, with a horrible wriggling movement of their entire body, and constantly surrounded by a cloud of pilot fish speeding about in every direction. The rays of light from our projectors, reddened with blood, the silvery flashing of the pilot fish, the sound of teeth scissoring into flesh, and the movements of these great gray and white forms, created a kind of horrible fantasia which seemed to go on forever. And yet, it was only a matter of five minutes and then everything was calm again. Even though the body of the dolphin was only half-devoured, his attackers had gone away and resumed their prudent circling. Some of them had even left the scene of the feast altogether, disappearing silently into the blackness of the sea. Only one remained behind, cautiously nibbling at his dead victim, taking bites that would have seemed insignificant a few moments before.

Their appetite is very quickly satiated, and a meal such as I have just described probably permits them to live for several weeks. But, for most sharks, this would be an exceptional repast. For those sharks that follow the great schools of cetaceans, it must be the habitual means of survival; once or twice a month, an ill or dead dolphin, and the rest of the time just the residue from births or other leavings. For those sharks that haunt the reefs and therefore do not have such a source of nourishment, there can be no precise answer to the question of their normal feeding habits. I have seen some fish attack others and fail to kill the intended victim, leaving him still swimming and trailing blood. And in every such case, a shark has appeared immediately and swallowed up whatever was left of the wounded animal. This occurs relatively frequently, since it is rare for a reef fish to pursue another if it escapes his first attack. In fact, the majority of such fish hunt in much the same way as a man hunting ducks; they simply lie in wait, protected by their blind of coral, until an imprudent visitor comes within reach. But if they fail in their initial assault, they are reluctant to follow the quarry into deeper waters, far from the protection of their coral hiding place. It is this moment of hesitation which provides opportunity for sharks or other predators from the open sea. It would certainly seem, therefore, that the favorite food and primary nourishment of sharks is fresh fish, and that sharks are capable of hunting for themselves.

After all, the occasions for seizing the would-be prey of another fish are not too frequent, sharks are comparatively numerous, and consequently they must go hunting. That their basic fare is fish might seem to contradict theories derived from the incredible list of objects found in the stomachs of captured sharks — objects ranging from canned goods to the remains of human arms and legs and other parts. Certain species of small sharks, with jaws particularly well adapted to this specific task, apparently feed on shellfish and crustaceans, which they crush between the flattened teeth lining both

The shark, *longimanus,* surrounded by his pilot fish eager for crumbs, takes a firm grip on the already torn flesh of the dead porpoise.

With the shark cage and the head of the diver in the right foreground, the shark now shakes his head from left to right with incredible violence to saw the piece of meat he is going to gulp.

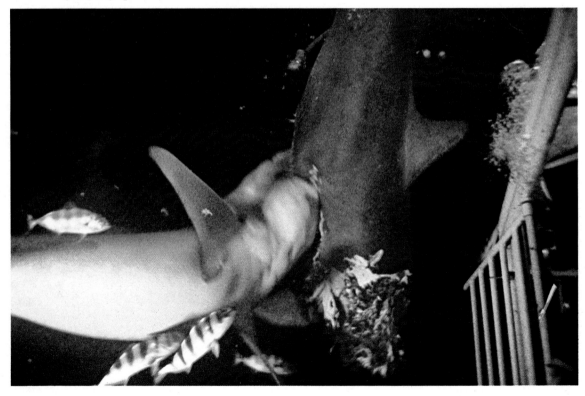

You can see the teeth, now erect, inside the mouth of the shark, tearing away at the carcass.

The diver is attempting to set out to tag the shark, which, needless to say, in this frenzied moment can be extremely dangerous. The diver is wearing his black-rubber light helmet. This complete sequence was shot at night about thirty feet below the Red Sea.

sides of their jaw. The majority of large sharks are extremely active predators, who survive on the leavings of the great schools of cetaceans or from a hunt of their own which may lead them to attack schools of very small fish. Such is the case with the thresher shark. What might be termed "terrestrial" flesh, such as that of a steer or a man, is doubtless not their favorite food, but they will eat it whenever they find it necessary.

In any case, few species of sharks, in comparison with their total numbers, are capable of seriously harassing man. In addition to the other sources of nourishment I have mentioned, sharks are known to feed on seals, turtles, and some sea birds. The largest species, the whale shark and the basking shark, feed exclusively on plankton, small fish, or small crustaceans, such as crayfish and red crabs. (There are some theories to the effect that these two last-named species of shark come to the surface only occasionally, which would explain the rarity of their sightings by seamen or fishermen.)

One of the most disagreeable experiences I have known in my years of diving was that of seeing a shark appear at a time when I had no means of protection in my hands. And yet, when I look back through the journals I kept on board ship, I constantly come across the notes I have made of such encounters: "Wednesday, December 7, — This morning, on a preliminary exploration, we dived on a little reef just north of the island of Malathu [in the Farasan Islands]. The coral here is small and stunted, somewhat resembling a heath or moor in the south of France. Many small, apparently timid, sharks haunted the beginning of the dive. Suddenly, from out of the depths beyond us, I saw three large *Albimarginatus* — seven to nine feet, I would guess — climbing toward us, swiftly and determinedly. They were far too large for me to contend with, especially on a free dive and with empty hands. I hastily signaled to the doctor, who was accompanying me, to get back to the *Zodiac,* and followed him as rapidly as I could. I managed to get aboard just as the sharks decided to launch their first attack."

It was episodes such as this that led us to devise our number one tool of protection — the "shark billy." In order to keep the shark at a distance without wounding and thereby angering him, we now always carry a staff of wood or aluminum, about three feet long and equipped at one end with a circle of small nails that grip the shark's skin and prevent him from simply slipping by it. The handle at the other end of the billy is provided with a loop, rather like that on a ski pole, so that it will not be wrenched from our hand by the shock of the attack. It is not in the least cumbersome to use, and although it is certainly not very impressive to look at, the billy is nonetheless very effective. It would be false to say that this device alone is adequate protection, since a shark thus turned away will almost invariably resume his patient circling and wait for another opportunity to attack. It is an exception to the rule if he allows himself to be so easily discouraged and simply swims away.

For this reason, and also because the most dangerous time in any encounter with a shark is the brief period in which the diver is attempting to leave the water and is temporarily blind, we almost never go down without the added protection of an antishark cage. Most of the time, it serves only as an elevator back to the surface, but in the event of danger it provides a shelter against any attack. We designed and built cages of all sizes and shapes before finally settling on two models. One type, capable of holding four divers, is approximately cubical in form, measuring seven feet in height by six and a half in width. The door opens in two sections, either from the top or the bottom, or both ways at once, if the work we are doing should require this. The other type of cage is almost spherical, with a trap door at the bottom and semicircles closing the top. It was designed for a single diver and can be used on the bottom, suspended from the ship, or by a diver propelling himself through the water by the movement of his legs, which project through the opened trap door. On many occasions we have been forced to make precipitous retreats to our cages, in order to avoid serious accidents. They also provide us with our only means of studying and filming the great shark frenzies while remaining in complete security ourselves. It was primarily for purposes of filming that we built la Balue, the plexiglass cage already mentioned, but although this type of cage is ideal for cinema use, it offers too great a resistance to water currents and tides and is too fragile for general use.

During the Second World War, the general staffs of all the world's armed forces evinced a growing interest in the study of sharks. Hundreds of sailors on torpedoed ships, as well as the pilots and crews of planes shot down over water, died horrible deaths because of sharks. This state of affairs caused great concern among the various military specialists and technicians, and there was good reason for it. As a single example, I might cite the following story:

At nine-fifteen on the morning of November 28, 1942, the British transport ship *Nova Scotia* was sunk by the torpedoes of a German submarine. The ship went down thirty miles off Cape St. Lucia, a promontory of the coast of Natal in South Africa. In addition to her crew, the *Nova Scotia* was carrying

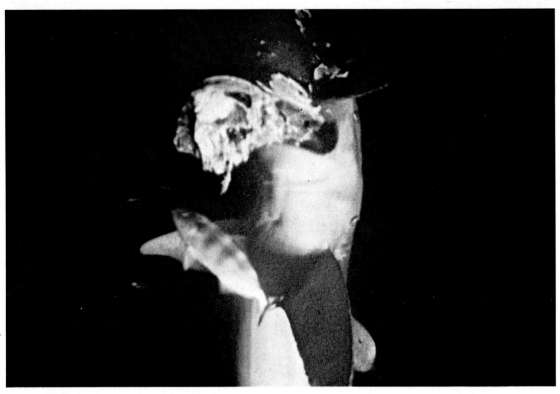

Now the shark has his mouth full of meat, tearing it to shreds.

He goes down, gulping his meat.

Another shark comes out, straight at the photographer. In the foreground you can see the hand of the diver, Serge Foulon, with his short tagging dagger in hand.

765 Italian prisoners of war and 134 South African soldiers, returning to Durban after having served in the Near East. Most of the lifeboats were destroyed in the explosion of the torpedoes, and hundreds of survivors were left with only their life belts or rafts of wood or rubber. One of the ultimate survivors of the disaster gave this account: "Suddenly, the ship was rocked by two terrible explosions, and we knew that we had been hit by torpedoes. I tried to reach my life belt, but the ship was already listing badly and I slipped in the oil and gasoline that covered the deck. I fell into the sea, wearing only a pair of swimming trunks. The water was covered with oil, but I swam until I found a floating spar and clung to that. Hundreds of men were swimming around me, clutching at rafts and other pieces of wreckage. Another soldier from my own regiment swam up and caught hold of the other end of the spar. He was wearing a life belt. We drifted all night. By dawn the next morning, the current had carried away the oil on the water, but we were still surrounded by other survivors. A little later, my companion told me that he thought it was better to die than to go on clinging to a piece of wood, with no hope of rescue. He said that he was going to let go, and refused to listen to me when I tried to change his mind. When I finally realized that my efforts were useless, I asked him to leave me his life belt. As he was unfastening the straps, he suddenly let out a horrible scream and the whole upper part of his body was lifted out of the water. When he fell back, the sea was red with blood and I could see that his lower leg had been cut off. At the same moment I saw the gray form of a shark swimming rapidly around him, and I got away from these as fast as I could. Then some sharks began to gather around me. They looked to be about six or seven feet long, and from time to time one of them would swim directly toward me. I clapped my hands in the water with all my strength, and that seemed to send them away. At last, I was able to reach one of the rafts and climb into it." Sixty hours after the submarine attack, the survivors were picked up by a Portuguese ship. A total of 192 persons were saved, but many of those who died were killed by sharks.

The effect of such stories on the morale of the men who fought in the air or on the sea was, understandably, disastrous. It was for this reason that many military laboratories in all parts of the world set to work to discover some effective means of protection against sharks. The final result, a discovery of the United States Naval Research Laboratory, was a small rectangular tablet containing a mixture of 20 per cent copper acetate and 80 per cent of a powerful deep-purple coloring substance. These ingredients were mixed with a wax which dissolved in water. The tablets were distributed to all personnel involved in operations on or above the water, and doubtless provided them with great moral support.

We tried out these "shark chaser" tablets during a series of dives in a depth of about one hundred feet, just off the Shab Arab Reef in the Gulf of Tadjoura, where the Red Sea and the Gulf of Aden come together. We lowered an installation made up of two cages facing each other, so that the cameraman in one cage could follow the movements and experiments of the two divers in the other. There were few sharks the first morning; the water was a trifle cloudy and carried along by a current of about a quarter of a knot. Serge Foulon opened a sack of fresh fish and released a few pieces to drift with the current. Almost at once, several silhouettes appeared in the milky depths. They were *Carcharhinus obscurus,* sharks with black-tipped fins, and averaging three to four feet in length. As soon as they were within easy range, José Ruiz opened his sack and freed the "shark chaser" tablet. It drifted four or five feet to the end of the attached ribbon and floated in the current, leaving behind it a thick, blackish smoke screen. As it dissolved, the dye expanded into swirling clouds, carried gently away from us by the movement of the water. A few minutes later, I saw six long and flexible forms tracking the path of dye and copper acetate just as dogs will track the source of a scent of roasting meat. They were large sand sharks, which weave through the water like serpents. One of them was more than fifteen feet in length — the largest sand shark I had ever seen. Although I knew them to be completely harmless, I instinctively recoiled at the sight of them. Serge, for his part, did not flinch and simply held out the tail of a barracuda to our new guests. The largest of the sand sharks scented first to the right and then to the left and at last came to nibble gently at the morsel of fish Serge was still holding. None of them seemed in the least bit disturbed by the "shark chaser," which still surrounded us in a thick, blue-black fog. We did not consider this first experiment satisfactory, so we set up another.

Before I went into the water, I watched Canoë Kientzy preparing what he called a "sandwich." He was slitting open some fresh fish and slipping into each of them a "shark chaser" tablet, stripped of its outer wrapping. When he had tied the whole sandwich back together, he attached it to the end of a long cord. I went down the ladder and into the water extremely cautiously, because we had sighted two *Albimarginatus,* more than six feet long and circling the ship in an apparent state of excitement. The moment I entered

the water they turned in my direction. I have already mentioned the unbelievable appearance of the shark when he is seen from directly in front.
Nothing remains of his beauty or his somewhat awkward grace. I could see
only the pointed snout and two wide-spaced eyes, the disturbing, faintly ridiculous swaying movement of his body, the symmetrical pectoral fins, and the
black line of his mouth against the lighter gray of his belly.

Turning, and swimming rapidly into the protection afforded by the two
propellers of the ship, I entered the waiting cage and half-closed its door. When
I signaled to Canoë, he tossed out the "sandwich," which came to rest just
about ten feet away from me. The moment it entered the water, the tablet
released its cloud of blue-black ink and the fish in which it was inclosed was
hidden from my view. The smaller of the two sharks began to move a trifle
more rapidly, turned brusquely away from the cloud of dye, then turned again,
swam back toward it and passed through it from one end to the other. When
he appeared, he had the sandwich in his mouth but was having trouble
swallowing it — doubtless because Canoë was still holding on to its length
of cord. Great, violet clouds were expelled from his gills with each of the
convulsive movements of his mouth and head, as he tried to rid himself of
the fish. At last, he succeeded in biting through the cord and swam away,
leaving behind him two separate clouds of purple dye. I could not prevent
myself from laughing hysterically, and the camera in my hands jumped up
and down. We would have to start all over. I knew this, but it was simply too
funny — seeing clouds of a product, which was supposed to repel a shark
and discourage him from biting, expelled from his gills like smoke from a
badly tuned motor.

We tried again. Second "sandwich," same result. In spite of the failure
of these experiments, however, I feel sure that copper acetate does nothing
to improve the digestion of the shark.

In many laboratories, and on the *Calypso,* all kinds of chemical products
have been tried, and all with the same lack of real success. They may work
with certain species of sharks, at certain times, but it is impossible to draw
any definite conclusions from these experiments. As for the American
"shark chaser" itself, we have tried it often, during all our voyages and under
extremely varying situations, but it has never yet been successful. The only
chemical substances which have a definite effect on sharks are so caustic that
they are dangerous to all organisms, including the human body.

Thus far, two types of barriers have been tested as protection for bathers

Our favorite means of transportation. The *Zodiac* allows us to go anywhere, jump into the water, climb back on board; this little boat carries as many as eight or nine people.

on beaches. One such system, which was tested by Australian authorities, consists of an electric screen in which two wires, one suspended from buoys close to the surface, and the other held on the bottom by weights, are maintained at a differing polarity. This system has seemed to be reasonably effective; several sharks have been observed to be either paralyzed or turned away. The Australian Government, however, has not felt that it was satisfactory. The price of installation was prohibitive and the infallibility of the system far from certain.

Another kind of barrier, made up of fine bubbles of air, also has had a temporary success. For several years, in fact, it was thought that man had found the ultimate weapon. Experiments conducted by Doctor Perry Gilbert have, however, demonstrated the uncertainties of this procedure. Experiments of more or less the same nature have also been carried out in South Africa. A tank twenty feet long, eight feet wide, and six feet deep was divided into

A different species of shark — the dusky shark, out in the open sea. This is the kind of shark we had when we tried the Johnson shark screen.

two sections by a pipe which was pierced with small openings and placed on the bottom. A compressor fed air into the pipe, so that it escaped through the holes and formed a curtain of fine bubbles, completely separating the two parts of the tank. Two series of experiments were then conducted, with a seven-foot *Carcharias taurus* and a six-foot *Carcharhinus obscurus*. In both series of tests, the barrier was formed while the sharks were at one end of the tank, and although the *Carcharhinus obscurus* remained on that side, the other shark began swimming very rapidly and passed through the barrier several times. In another series, when a wounded but still living fish was placed in the water on the side of the tank separated from the sharks, both animals crossed through the barrier within a matter of seconds and attacked the other fish.

Some divers claim that exhaling a large breath of air in the direction of an approaching shark will cause him to flee. The procedure will succeed with the majority of inoffensive sharks, but these species tend to avoid any encounter with a diver, so the efficacy of the system is, at least, open to question. I have employed it myself, with sharks of the dangerous species — tiger sharks and blue sharks, for example — without ever finding it successful. Moreover, in the course of our many dives, I have seen sharks pass with complete indifference through the large clouds of air bubbles emanating from my companions' breathing equipment.

The procedures for the self-protection of the diver that have been tried out at one time or another are numerous and varied, ranging from cartridges of dynamite to compressed-air-driven harpoons and including such devices as ultrasonic generators, extracts of spoiled meats, and electrical discharges. We have tested many of them, and found that the majority are ineffective, some extremely doubtful, and others too cumbersome for the diver. There is, however, one that merits attention, the Johnson "shark screen," which we termed "Johnson's bucket," because of its peculiar shape. We experimented with it near the reef surrounding Dahl Ghab island.

At first, the device seemed ridiculous to us. It is a kind of buoy, formed of three superimposed inflatable rings, to which is attached a large pouch of waterproof plastic about six and a half feet deep. When the upper part has been inflated, the shipwrecked individual (or the experimenter, in our case) settles himself into the "bucket" thus formed and fills it with water until it attains its full size. In this manner, he is floating in a waterproof, cylindrical enclosure, which isolates him from the water around him. It is a far more

The most familiar aspect of the shark: seen through the surface—the very sinuous shape coming toward the boat, searching lazily, with the dorsal fin and the caudal fin skimming the surface. This is the sight that has frightened generations of sailors and so many bathers. This is the sight for which guards scan the waters from the lookout towers of Australia and South Africa so that they can warn bathers and divers of the perilous sharks' whereabouts. It is a characteristic shape, but people often mistake this shape for that of a dolphin or a large fish.

rational device than it might seem at first glance. For one thing, when the whole "shark screen" is deflated and folded, it is not at all cumbersome; and for another, perhaps more important, no scent can filter through to the shark, and he does not have a visual sighting of arms and legs beating at the water.

Several sharks were swimming around the motionless *Calypso* when I first descended cautiously into the orange circle of the buoy. I filled the dark-green pouch immediately, and clung with one hand to the hook of our hydraulic crane. By following this procedure, I could be lifted rapidly from the water in case of attack. It was a new impression for me, and not at all agreeable, to be situated with my head just out of the water and unable to follow the movements of the sharks on the choppy surface. I no longer felt any desire to laugh at sharks snapping up fish baited with tablets of copper acetate.

The shark nearest to me was no more than a grayish blur of changing shape, slipping in and out of focus. He turned, very close to me, quite obviously interested in the shark screen and its occupant. I raised my head and tried to lift my neck and shoulders above the surface, hoping that I could then see more clearly. Once, I felt the rasp of his body against the plastic of the pouch, followed almost immediately by the shock of his flicking tail. Several times, he passed so close to me that I could have reached out and touched his fin. My left hand was still gripping the hook of the crane so tightly that the knuckles were white with strain.

Canoë Kientzy was watching the experiment from one of our small boats nearby. He was armed with a high-powered rifle, but that reassured no one. The plastic material of which the cockpit was made — as thin and fine as paper — swung back and forth to the movement of the waves, and I found it difficult not to interrupt this natural movement with inconsidered kicking of my feet.

To complete the experiment, I decided now to try to attract the shark toward me. I slapped at the water with the palm of my hand, and at the same time some fresh fish bait was thrown into the water from the ship. At last, the big shark started straight toward me, moving fast and determinedly, and I promptly gave the signal to be hauled aboard. Still clinging to the cable of the crane, I looked down and saw him pass, six feet below my dangling legs but well away from the empty shark screen. A false alarm — he was attacking the bait, not me.

In a later experiment, we put a whole flotilla of these Johnson buckets in the water. Doctor Millet, Jacques Renoir, Serge Foulon, Claude Templier, and Marcel Soudre each occupied one, while René Aaron manned a rifle in the *Zodiac* to assure their security. Canoë and I planned to film the reactions of the sharks from beneath. There were two large, gray sharks, about seven feet in length and with small pectoral fins, thinly bordered with black on their lower surface. Their manner of swimming was supple, slow, and sinuous; and their hollow bellies attested to the degree of their hunger. Another pair of sharks was scarcely visible, very far below. I lifted my head above water and listened for a moment to the slightly caustic pleasantries being exchanged by our guinea pigs. Then I dived again.

Beneath the surface, I was again confronted with an unimaginable spectacle. In the universe of the unreal, where the silver light of the sun cleaves the deep blue of the sea, the two sharks above me seemed to be swimming at the center of the green pockets. They lazed through and among these lifeless, odorless objects, and then, with no hesitation, they both turned and launched themselves directly at Canoë, who repelled them with great sweeps of his shark billy. Returning at once to their earlier state of indolence, they abandoned my "bodyguard" and turned on me, hoping, perhaps, that I might prove an easier prey. When I had climbed back into the *Zodiac,* I repictured the scene in my mind and came to the conclusion that Mr. Johnson's shark screens have a good future.

I do not believe that these screens could be effective against a shark in a frenzy of hunger, but the chances are not large that a shipwrecked person, or a man or woman landing in the ocean from a disabled plane, would encounter such a situation. For my part, I think that Mr. Johnson's buoys can very definitely increase the possibility of survival of anyone alone on the high seas. One point, however, should be made: the plastic material is extremely fragile, and anything can tear it open, so due caution should be observed with such things as belt buckles, shoes, and watches.

Confronted with the ineffectiveness of traditional methods of self-protection employed by divers, we have settled on a technique that has often saved us in tricky situations. Instead of crying out under water or blowing clouds of air bubbles or plunging straight toward any shark of menacing appearance — methods which have no practical effect — we practice what we call back-to-back defense. Since we had already arrived at the principle of never diving alone, there is always a minimum of two, and in case of danger, far from a protective cage, we place ourselves back-to-back, with each man using one hand to hold on to the diving suit of the other. In this position, each man can effectively defend a sector that does not exceed his angle of vision. And of course we never dive without having a protective instrument of some kind in our hands. In waters in which we are likely to encounter sharks, we carry either a shark billy or a camera.

The one thing of importance that emerges from this brief summary of the various means of protection against sharks is that none of those actually in use, with the exception of the cumbersome steel antishark cage, is absolutely sure. The further we advance in our knowledge of sharks, the more evident becomes the futility of any attempt to understand them completely. Their reactions are unpredictable, and ordinary statistics are of no value. I have seen hundreds of sharks follow the same technique in approaching to attack and bite, and yet, on some occasions, they have surprised me by attacking in a completely different manner. It goes without saying that the greatest prudence is always necessary, but it should be prudence based on respect and not on contempt.

EIGHT:
The Island of Derraka
The narrow escape
of Dr. François.
Individual cages.
Battling a swarm
of little sharks.

Philippe Cousteau's narrative continues

A catastrophic week passed by. Every afternoon, the haboob, that violent storm of burning sand, beat down on the ship and prevented us from working. At about two o'clock, the sky above the western horizon would turn a reddish-gold and the sea would cease to live, its surface becoming absolutely motionless, seeming almost solid. The already stifling temperature became intolerable; our bodies ran with sweat and every movement was torture, aggravated by the rash of prickly heat with which we were all afflicted. Then the storm was on us and the howling wind raised little spouts of water that mingled with the sand and covered everything with a coating of yellowish, destructive mud. Since we had gotten under way at the first signs of the approaching storm, we were usually anchored in the shelter of some small island when it actually struck. As soon as it became possible to work again, we were forced to put in what seemed interminable hours of meticulous cleaning, in order to protect our delicate and valuable equipment. Our eyes red and swollen, we moved about like automatons in a sandy, unbearable universe.

These difficult days undermined the morale of the crew, caused deterioration of matériel, and finally made it necessary for us to put in at Massawa, the capital of Eritrea, for a premature overhaul. My father decided to take the *Calypso* in, without losing any more time in these waters. Canoë and I succeeded in persuading him to leave us on a deserted island farther out at sea, with enough supplies for a week, and with equipment making it possible for us to get some work accomplished. The time remaining to us to complete our film and our study of sharks seemed very short to me, and I was eager to try to make up for all the days lost to us by the wretched sandstorms.

After a rapid exploration of a half-dozen isolated scraps of sand, we selected the island of Derraka in the Suakin group. We decided on the location of our camp and then set to work at once to open a more or less navigable passage for our small boats through the belt of water-level coral that surrounded that Red Sea island. The team to be left behind was made up of Canoë, Doctor François, Serge Foulon, and Raymond Deloire. Raymond was a still photographer and the brother of our excellent chief operator, Michel Deloire. I accompanied them, of course, to do the filming.

When we had brought our equipment ashore and set up the tent, we returned to the *Calypso* for a little "farewell" dinner prepared for us by Jean Morgan. In the course of this dinner, we worked out a precise program of what

This is our camp on Derraka Island. Despite the brightness, it is approximately four o'clock in the morning. The photographer is Raymond Deloire. Pictured in the foreground, sleeping on the red-and-blue mattress, is Canoë. Next to him, still wrapped in his sheet, is Foulon. Standing is our doctor, and Philippe is reading a book, or trying to catch a few more minutes of sleep, on the low cot next to the tent.

This is the island's lagoon just in front of the camp. The photographer is positioned in front of our tent for this shot. On the left you can see our compressors. They are air compressors used to recharge our tanks. The equipment right in front of us, with a can of oil and gasoline, is used for the outboard motor. One of the launches on the beach is the security launch, the one we will use only in case of emergency—for example, in the event the *Zodiac* encounters engine trouble outside the lagoon area; the strong currents could make it impossible for the *Zodiac* to return, forcing it to drift for miles and miles. Possibly a light wind could haul it way out of reach. Radioing the always ready security launch would bring help instantaneously, and the situation would be under control within a short while.

The birds along the shore are feeding on remnants of the fish we cleaned in that area for dinner. Two people are spending this exasperatingly hot hour of the day in the cooler water of the lagoon. That is the place where Doctor François was endangered by a sand shark. Every day from 10 A.M. to 2 P.M., or even longer, the water provided us with relief from the unbearable heat of the sun.

we wanted to accomplish during our stay on the island. First of all, a study of the small sharks of the sand flats, then a continuous surveillance of a portion of the coral cliffs, with the idea of forming a kind of census of the visitors from the open sea who came here in search of nourishment. And, of course, we also planned to ignore no aspect of the life existing on this desolate strip of sand itself.

At last we said goodby to the others, with a handshake that may have been a trifle more formal than was our custom. Although, in theory, we were running no particular risk, the stay of a group as small as ours on an isolated island in the Red Sea is not exactly a picnic. In case of an accident, we were far from any surgical equipment; and in the unlikely case of a visit from any mainland natives, we would have been at their mercy. I promised myself to allow no one to risk anything that seemed in the least uncertain, especially where sharks were concerned. The *Calypso* drew away from the shore and was rapidly lost to sight in the gathering darkness. In what seemed just a moment, only the sound of her engines still came to us across the becalmed sea.

That first night, I was the only one that seemed interested in anything but rest. The *Calypso* had scarcely disappeared before my companions wrapped themselves in sheets and slept, exhausted by this day of excitement and activity. Left alone, I walked slowly down to the water. I had the curious impression of approaching some secret rendezvous with my dreams. There was no moon, and yet everything shone with a mysterious light that seemed to emanate from the landscape itself, rather than being simply reflected by the objects it struck. I had no tendency even toward thinking or meditation; I just watched and listened, without understanding, perhaps somewhat as an animal does. The water of the lagoon was warm and alive, rustling with the sound of thousands of claws and tiny legs, of microbattles, and of scurryings back and forth. As is true in most tropical seas, a fluorescent stream of light flashed across the water at the sudden move of a fish. On the beach, every wave traced a drawing different from all the others and then was erased a moment later, leaving not even a memory. At the water's edge, innumerable armies of hermit crabs maneuvered to the rhythm of some incomprehensible logic. Since I was standing motionless, everything took place very close around me. A crab went by, trailing a live and feeble chick, doubtless stolen from one of the sea-swallow's nests which covered the island. They passed within inches of my foot, and disappeared into a hole in the sand I had not seen. A little ten- or twelve-inch sand shark was swimming at the very limits of the water, searching for small shellfish or for crabs, whose exit from the water he would block with his own body.

I was torn away from my silent communion with nature by the sound of voices coming from the camp, and hurried back there as rapidly as possible. Millions of hermit crabs had invaded the camp area and were climbing across the bodies of the sleepers they had so unexpectedly awakened. For the next hour, we stood and watched as this multitude of tiny creatures emerged from the edges of the scraggy bush behind us and passed by on their way to the sea. It was a journey of almost two hundred feet which, for them, might require an hour or more. They climbed over or detoured around every obstacle they

Some distance away from the *Calypso,* visible at the right, are the two launches; one of them is moored and the other is going to be docked with it. We are about to drop the cages overboard into the little cove where sharks had been spotted that morning. It is a small bay, set between two coral heads bearing the whitest sand at the bottom. This is to be a tagging operation.

Some of our shark cages are portable aluminum cages. The small round shapes on top are floats. A cage is floating on the water when the diver enters. The diver brings with him a lead weight, which causes the cage slowly to submerge. While submerging, the diver attaches the weight to the bottom of the cage, thus enabling him to free both hands for his work. One of the prime advantages of the portable cage is the fact that it is neutral in water, enabling the diver to steer it by opening the rear door, sticking his legs out, and swimming with it in the direction of his choice. In order to surface, all the diver has to do is dump the weight, thus causing the contraption to rise slowly to the surface.

In this picture Doctor François is on the right, with Jean-Paul Bassaget, center, holding a cage. Philippe Cousteau is driving the launch. The second launch is occupied by Canoë Kientzy, Jacques-Yves Cousteau (a towel in his hand), and Marcel Soudre in the rear.

It is now time to get into the water after a last reading of the available light topside proves favorable. The reading will be rechecked underwater for filming.

came to, and there were obstacles everywhere. This gigantic nightly migration was not the exclusive property of our campsite; it took place along the whole length of the beach on this side of the island. The tidal wave of scurrying little animals eventually disappearing into the water was an extraordinary spectacle — and I never saw them carry out the same mass procedure in reverse.

In the days that followed, we acquired the habit of not retiring until after the passage of this clicking, clattering wave. I think, personally, that all the hermit crabs awaited a certain degree of obscurity, toward the end of the afternoon, before beginning their descent to the sea. I would see them gathering along the edges of the thorny bushes which cover the central part of the island. In compact clusters, they would wait for dusk, the shock of their shells forming a continuous rustling sound as they brushed against each other. On their return, they must have come back at differing times, in accordance with whatever luck they had had in accomplishing whatever need it was that took them to the water — reproduction or simply feeding. Thus, when they returned across the beach, one by one, they went unnoticed.

On the day after our first experience with the crabs, we explored the island from one end to the other, setting out very early, before the heat of the sun made such movement impossible. The island is elongated and a trifle narrower at its center than it is at either end. It is oriented roughly from northeast to southwest, and surrounded by a sandbank forming a lagoon several times larger than the island itself. It is covered with a thorny vegetation having very small dark-green leaves, and its center forms a shallow and slightly less arid valley, which we christened The Happy Valley. Obviously, there is not a drop of fresh water on the entire island, and yet life abounds on it. We have visited dozens of islands like this and my companions are bored with them. But it is always a source of wonder to me that these shelves of arid sand, lost in the saline furnace of the Red Sea, could form a refuge for a secret, but dense and bustling form of life. It is primarily the birds which dominate the life of the island, peopling it with their cries and movement, and sometimes also with the brilliance of their colors. And in this universe, the sea eagles reign as unquestioned masters. Using twigs and bits of driftwood, they construct mounds which may rise anywhere from three to ten feet in height. The nests which crown these artificial hillocks are always filled with feathers, bones, and, especially, the remains of dead fish. I once saw a sea eagle fishing on the sandbank of the island of Marmar in the northern Farasan group. The bird hovers motionless above the water and then, like all other birds of prey, he drops like a stone, claws stretched out toward his intended victim. In the case of the sea eagle, the prey may be protected by as much as two feet of water and the bird will vanish into it completely for a fraction of a second before laboriously rising again. Through strength alone, he frees himself of the water and climbs slowly to a height of a hundred or so feet, where he seems to pause to shake out his plumage, forming a shower of tiny rainbows, and then flies on to rest on the sand. The body and legs of this bird are completely inadapted to swimming, and the force by which he succeeds in lifting himself free of the water, simply through the power of his wings, is a magnificent thing to see. His island domain provides him with everything he needs to feed himself and his young, until the day arrives when he chases them off, to preserve the balance of the realm and his own supremacy.

The sea eagle is not the only bird of prey in this territory, however. There also exists a species of small blue-gray hawks, which I saw for the first time on Derraka and have never seen on the islands on the other side of the Red Sea. I think this is due to the presence on the islands of the Suakin group of many small rodents, which provide nourishment for the hawks. They bear a strong resemblance to large martins, having the same elongated wings and the same acrobatic manner of flight.

In the springtime, the sea swallows come to lay their eggs and hatch their young, while the solan geese (perhaps more commonly known as the booby gannet) take possession of the island in November and December, for the same reasons. In both cases, the island is literally covered with eggs and then with the grayish forms of baby chicks; the air vibrates constantly with their strident cries, and countless battles take place. Some red-beaked gulls survey these immense nurseries attentively, hoping to snatch up a helpless chick or an egg; they will break the egg by dropping it on the rocks, and then consume its contents.

It was on Derraka that I saw to what extent man's intrusion destroys the fragile equilibrium of natural life. Our arrival on the island had disturbed the swallows around the campsite, so they had left their nests temporarily and had probably not been able to find them again in the darkness. As a result, a swarm of ocypode crabs had descended on the nests in a murderous raid and carried off many of the chicks, which were still too weak to defend themselves. As I had seen on that same night, the dawn surprised a great many crabs hastily dragging off the newborn birds.

On another occasion, as I was walking very cautiously between the eggs of a nursery of baby swallows, I noticed that the sea swallows feared my presence more than a few gulls that followed close behind me. As a result of this, a circle formed around me in which the young were no longer protected by their parents. The gulls, knowing more of the situation than I, profited from it to steal several chicks, despite the furious cries of the swallows circling in the sky not far away. I could not help but wonder why the gulls had waited for such a unique opportunity. They were much larger and stronger than the little swallows, so it seemed to me that they could have helped themselves to what they wanted at any time they chose. The explanation lies in the fact that the gulls are not at all numerous in this region, and each time one of them approaches a nest a swarm of swallows attacks him and forces him to retreat. By frightening the swallows more than the gulls, my presence had upset this balance of forces. But even so, the gulls had great difficulty in leaving the involuntary protective circle I had created for them, and most of them could only escape the confines of this menacing circumference at the price of losing their prey.

I have never attempted to protect one animal against another, and our arrival in this microcosm of a world was no less natural than would have been a cataclysm of any other kind. When, on occasion, I have caught myself in the act of qualifying one animal as "good" and another as "bad," I have been tempted to laugh. I have seen storms reduce the population of entire islands to nothing, sweeping off all life in a few hours. Our sole ambition, on the *Calypso,* is to maintain the natural sequence of events, in the presence of humans. In other words, not to indulge in the useless, gratuitous massacre which is termed hunting for sport. Our needs in fresh fish for nourishment are generally satisfied by fishing, and only rarely by underwater hunting. And hunting as a land sport is almost unknown among the members of our crew.

At the northern end of the island, we came across an accumulation of empty shells and red madrepore, gathered together in an unusual shape. It was a Moslem tomb, oriented to the northeast, in the direction of Mecca and the tomb of the Prophet. The mound seemed to have been built in the form of a ship, with two large pieces of coral planted vertically at either end, to represent the prow and the stern. The comrades of the man who was guiding this ship on its longest journey had adorned it with all the flowers of the sea. All the care of the gravediggers could be read in the area surrounding this final resting place. They had dug up and flattened out a mound of fine sand, bordered with tufts of dried coral, now white as bones. Shells, possibly left as offerings, had been piled more than three feet high and decorated with fragments of multi-colored bottles, with here and there a red splash of Tubipora coral. The man had probably been a pilgrim, herded with others from the African coast into

Below the anchored launches, divers are swimming down to their respective cages. One of the one-man cages is in the foreground. The photographer's cage is sitting in the background. The figures at the surface are observers swimming. We must get the cages positioned before we enter.

No sharks are yet in sight as this picture is taken. When they finally appeared, however, there were many. Michel Deloire was filming.

The look on Serge's face shows the state of mind we experienced during those dives; anything could happen and we had to be extremely cautious.

a small sailing vessel and succumbing later to the terrible conditions of the voyage. Or perhaps he was one of those old nakhodas who presided over the destinies of these coastal vessels, seated motionless at the center of their ship until they died. They commanded the young fishermen who gathered shells for mother-of-pearl and caught a few fish for their food.

Everywhere we went, the land seemed pock-marked, riddled with subterranean galleries which collapsed beneath our feet, revealing burrows no larger than a man's thumb. At first, it seemed that this might be one of the effects of the infernal heat, but we later discovered the real nature of this underground network. One night, after the regular migration of the hermit crabs, we were invaded by the mice. They were scarcely more than an inch in length, but their numbers were incredible and they attacked everything in sight. Their sudden presence stunned us for a moment, but then we immediately began looking for some means of shelter for all our perishable goods, either by hanging them from poles or enclosing them in waterproof cases. It was this invasion that supplied me with the answer to the presence on Derraka of the blue-gray hawks. I still do not know whether the leaves on the bushes provide water to quench the thirst of the tiny rodents themselves, but the next morning we found all our water bottles filled with their dead bodies. They had been able to enter through the necks of the bottles, but once inside they had drowned, because they were incapable of climbing out of their glass prison. For our own needs, we now had only one keg of water, containing less than twenty gallons.

Our exploration of the island had taken up the entire morning, and at about eleven o'clock, when the heat and the sun became unbearable, we hastily consumed a slice of grilled tuna and then went into the water. We stayed there, paddling idly about, until three-thirty, by which time it was again possible to support the furnacelike heat.

Every day thereafter, we spent the hottest hours comfortably immersed in the lagoon, wearing wide-brimmed hats to protect our faces. Doctor François regaled us with interminable and very funny stories, and the early afternoon hours passed in an atmosphere of gaiety and enforced idleness. Outside the water, the temperature would have read ninety-eight degrees in the shade — if there had been any shade. But there was nothing but the dazzling white sand, whose reflection, added to the sunlight, would have burned our bodies to a crisp in a few hours.

It was during one of these required bathing periods that Doctor Francois was attacked by a shark. Our work usually began at four o'clock in the morning, and after we had finished and had a rapid meal we went to an area just at the edge of the beach where the water averaged only two to three feet in depth. The water here in the lagoon was refreshing enough, although quite warm, but as one drew closer to the outer reef surrounding the island, the water became agreeably cool. On the second day, Jo — as we all called the doctor — began walking through the water toward the outer side of the lagoon. Suddenly, he disappeared from our sight and there was a great splashing of water, in the midst of which we could clearly make out the tail of a large shark. We were racing across the lagoon when Jo reappeared, very calmly, and a shadowy form flitted across the length of the outer reef and vanished in the distance. Jo explained what had happened, in fewer words than he normally used for one of his stories: he had been walking along slowly when the sand beneath his feet had suddenly erupted, much as if a rug had been pulled out from under him. In spite of his surprise and the confusion in the water, he had then made out the shape of a shark, which had turned back toward him and then, for no apparent reason, turned again and gone away.

This is by no means an unusual story, and many people have been surprised by sand sharks in the same conditions. Some have even been seriously bitten. A sand shark only three to four feet in length possesses a jaw that is quite sufficient to bite off a respectable piece of anything it attacks, and although its teeth may be small they are no less sharp for that.

That same evening we made a night dive, to try out our underwater floodlights and, if possible, to gather enough lobsters for a meal. Along the reefs of the Red Sea and the Indian Ocean, lobsters come out only at night. Invisible during the day, they hide in deep holes in the protective coral, to escape their enemies. Night, by depriving these predators of their normal resources, becomes day for the lobsters, who emerge from their shelters and hunt through the sand and coral in search of food. On the island of Abu Latt, in the Farasan group, I have even seen some who came completely out of the water to cross an obstructing coral peak.

Six feet beneath the surface, the beam of our lights brushed across tufts of coral bursting with unsuspected color. Fish with great, staring eyes remained frozen in place, as if paralyzed by the ray of some science-fiction weapon. They drew away slowly, and it was even possible to reach out and caress the iridescent scales. (These nocturnal adventures always give me the feeling of being a slightly mad magician. My light is a magic wand, capable both of creating fantasies and of destroying them. When I flick the switch, I am still dazzled and find myself back in the darkness of a void. Flick it again, and I am in the midst of a fantasia of anarchic creations, independent of me.

This one is a white-tip reef shark moving in the night. Its shape is disquieting in those dark hours. François's projector provided the lighting.

A night shot of a shark as it appears in the distance. The diver in the foreground has his eye on the killer and will try not to lose sight of him, or he would really be in trouble. Chances are, however, the diver will retreat to the reef and stay hidden among the coral heads.

Sometimes I swim very fast, sometimes slowly, often lying on my back, looking up into the mirror of the surface as my visions appear, explode, and vanish in the thin shaft of my light.) A short distance away, Jo seemed bathed in the aura of his projector, as if he were caught in a multicolored spider's web. Like myself, he was reaching out to the motionless fish, his movements reflecting his astonishment at this artificial familiarity with animals who normally fled at the sight of us. We were the St. Francis of the fish.

Suddenly, it was over. My magic beam had lost its power, and irradiated nothing but the void. We had arrived at the edge of the outer reef, where an absolutely vertical cliff plunged down to a depth of over six hundred feet. The water in front of us now was black and empty. Clinging to the last tufts of coral, we tried to search the depths with our fast-weakening projectors.

It was the beam from my light that picked up the reef shark. He was a very large reef shark, about twelve feet long, and he was slowly swimming up the river of light. When he arrived at what he apparently considered a reasonable distance from its source, he swerved lazily and began gliding toward me. The reflections of light on his body were almost silvery, and his eyes, with their contracted pupils, seemed tiny spots of black. The narrow shaft of my light threw all his scars into sharp relief, like some sinister form of tattoo. Little threads of flesh dangled from a recent cut at the corner of his mouth. But, somehow, there was an astonishing impression of purity in his movements and in his form, etched as it was in silver against the total blackness of the night. For a moment or two, he patrolled the edge of the cliff, then plunged straight down and disappeared.

I was frightened now, certain that he had not really gone, that he was swimming somewhere around us, his unmoving little eye still fixed on us. The night was filled with disturbing shapes, and in our efforts to see in every direction, the fading beams of our lamps danced an incoherent ballet. I was invaded by a feeling of total impotence; the water which a moment before had been so gentle had now become an enemy, armed with an unknown and hostile life. Our projectors, and all the technical progress they represented, were no more than futile playthings that we vainly brandished like arrogant Prometheuses. We had thought ourselves capable of chasing off the night with our tiny sparks. But the night remained, immense and solid. In a night dive on a reef such as this, as soon as one moves about too much, becomes uneasy, and loses absolute self-control, one's movements may precipitate one against the fiery, razoredged peaks of coral that inflict thousands of small but painful scratches and wounds. At last, my light picked up another slender form. It was a shark, not the one we had seen before, smaller, but seeming no less formidable. But now I had escaped the hypnotic sorcery of the night and was aware of our danger. Jo and I, watching each other closely, began to swim back toward the beach. When we were halfway there, we came across the *Zodiac*. Canoë had thought it wise to follow us, and assure us of an immediate exit from the water in case of danger. We collapsed in the bottom of the boat, not speaking, listening to the murmurs of the night.

The silvery image of that great shark haunted me through the rest of the night, even though I knew that the constant, vigilant patrol did not cease with darkness. I have said before that sharks, unlike most other fish, do not possess a swimming bladder that would permit them to float in equilibrium at any level of water. If a shark ceases to swim, he sinks slowly to the bottom. He is thus forced to live in a state of constant movement. Some fishermen, in regions where sharks are particularly abundant, have tried to capture them with explosions of dynamite. It is a completely impracticable system, since a shark killed in this manner will never rise to the surface. This factor, added to the absence of respiratory muscles in their systems, forces sharks to swim unceasingly, day and night, in search not only of food but of vital oxygen. It is a searching that may last for more than thirty years.

I went to sleep at last on the sand of the beach, thinking of this creature condemned to eternal journeying, to the incessant caress of water against his body, to an implacable, unending love affair with the sea.

Before we left our island, the *Calypso* rejoined us, to take part in a last experiment. With the help of Paul Zuéna, our first mate, we installed a complicated marking setup in a passage through the reef. We placed the large cage, to be used by the film cameraman, on a floor of white sand at the bottom of a wide fault. On either side of the entrance to this cage and at a slightly greater depth, there were two smaller cages for the banderilleros, the divers with the marking devices. At the center of the stage thus set, we placed transparent spherical plastic traps containing bits of fresh fish. In addition to this, each of the two smaller cages carried a sack containing more small pieces of fish. On the surface, my father was in one of the small boats, from which he could direct the entire operation, and Raymond Deloire was in another, prepared to photograph events from this angle.

At about two o'clock, the whole setup was in place and the program began, with a large distribution of fish. Serge Foulon was in the small cage to the left of the entrance and I was in the one to the right. Michel Deloire, with the film camera, was in the large cage, protected by Canoë, who was armed with a long, solid shark billy. A reconnaissance team we had sent out in the morning had reported a considerable number of fairly large sand and reef sharks in the area, so I expected to see them appear momentarily in the turning from the cliff, attracted by the sounds we had made and by the scent of fresh fish. I was somewhat deceived when I saw only one, then two, and then two more very small sharks, no longer than my arm, swimming rapidly and apparently nervous. But this deception did not last long. One after another, more than fifteen sharks suddenly appeared, excited, scenting the atmosphere like a pack of wolves.

Many divers ridicule these small sharks, considering them easily frightened and not worthy of concern. They are generally right in this opinion, but only if the sharks are alone or in very small groups. These same divers are likely to reckon that a man faced with a vicious dog is in far greater danger. Personally, I prefer dogs; there is almost always some way to outmaneuver them — unless they have been trained by man to attack. A shark less than three feet long can quite easily tear a foot or a hand from an overconfident diver. Its jaws are larger than those of any dog, its teeth much sharper and perfectly adapted to slice a limb in two.

I glanced toward Michel, in the large cage. He seemed as disappointed as I had been, and ready to return to the surface, so I signaled to him to wait. Serge, as impassive as ever, was preparing his spear for marking. Within a few minutes, the pack that had now gathered had burst the plastic traps and the fish inside had been completely devoured. I recognized some small blackfinned sharks and a few of the sinuous sand sharks. Our little arena was filled with them. They were all swimming very fast, and seemed to rebound from the walls of multicolored coral like bullets from a rifle. I realized that the scent of fish must by now have penetrated the whole of this relatively enclosed space, making any detection of its source of origin almost impossible and thereby exciting them even further.

It occurred to me suddenly that sharks as small as these could pass between the bars of our cages, and this is precisely what happened. Two of the little demons slipped into my cage and thrashed about between my legs, attempting to reach the sack of fish, which they had finally found. For several seconds, I kicked at them like a jackass, trying to force them out, and when I had succeeded in this I set to work to rid myself of the sack. Even as I fought off new attempts at entrance with great slaps of my open hands against the bars, I tried to detach the plastic bag, but I could not do it. Cursing at José, who had thought he was doing a good job in attaching it so solidly, I unsheathed the little dagger that formed the handle of my shark billy, but it had not been sharpened and would not cut well enough to sever the nylon cords of the fastening. All around me now, a carrousel of little sharks was engaged in a frenzied saraband. They bit at everything within reach, including the bars of the cage, shaking them between their teeth like mad dogs. Serge seemed to be having the same problems, but out of the corner of my eye I caught a glimpse of Michel, calmly registering it all on film.

A shark succeeded in penetrating the roof of the cage, and while I battled with him, a blow of his tail displaced my face mask, depriving me of vision. Now I was beginning to be overwhelmed by a feeling of frustrated rage. I was not going to be torn to pieces in this idiotic cage by these little brutes. I managed to readjust my face mask, emptying it of water with a great blast of air, and then opened the upper door of the cage. Kicking with my feet and lashing out with my hands, I got out at last and reached the shelter of the big cage, standing with my back to it and facing out toward the enemy. But as soon as I left the little cage, the sharks abandoned me and became entirely concerned with the sack of fish. In this moment of calm, I watched as they tore it apart and swallowed its contents. Serge, who had succeeded in ridding himself of his sack almost at the beginning, had remained in his cage and even managed to carry out several fine markings.

At the entrance to the bottleneck of our passage through the reef, several large forms cruised back and forth, but made no attempt to enter. The great sharks had refused the invitation to our party; we had underestimated their reluctance to enter enclosed areas. On the surface above us, my father was swimming slowly around his boat. It was he who had made possible my flight by tossing out bits of fish not far from my cage, attracting the majority of the little sharks toward an easier prey.

When I came up, I was furious about the way the experiment had developed, but all the others laughed about it so heartily that I soon found myself joining with them. For a long time thereafter, the men of the ship would ask me to explain how it came about that I had grown so fond of sharks that I carried one under each arm inside my cage.

It was the first time that sharks of such small size had been a real danger, but it was not to be the last, as I was able to testify at the time of the terrible frenzy at Shab Arab.

NINE:
Frenzy at Shab Arab
Arrival at
Shab Arab Reef.
A terrible mass frenzy.
The killing of a shark
and its effects.

Philippe Cousteau's narrative continues

The bottom appeared as a black line on the sensitized paper of the powerful echo sounder. Several of us were gathered around my father, watching the delicate tracing as it sloped gently upward. The total silence which reigned on the *Calypso's* bridge was broken only by the calm voice of JYC* giving his orders, and the voice of the helmsman as he repeated them.

Jean-Paul Bassaget, our first lieutenant, was transcribing the meanderings of our route onto the chart before him. It was night, and Canoë's face, as he leaned over my father's shoulder, reflected the slightly reddish glow of the instruments on the control panel.

"Right one five."

"The helm is right one five."

I was aware of a slight vibration as the ship veered a trifle to starboard. We were about to open up a new sector of the reef of Shab Arab.

"Hold her steady."

"Steady as she goes, Commandant."

"What is our heading?"

"One three zero, Commandant."

"Keep her at one three zero."

"Yes, Commandant."

*My father was always referred to by his initials — JYC — in a name that would sound rather like "Jeek" in English.

In the moment of renewed silence, my father changed the scale of sensitivity of the echo sounder to increase the precision of the graph, and the recorder began to turn more rapidly, giving out an almost imperceptible rasping sound. I knew that, inside the earphones, the slight tapping of the departing beams and the echo from the reflection on the bottom were mingled with the sounds of water against the hull. The graph on the paper showed that the bottom was no more than twenty-five feet beneath our keel.

"Come down to plot five, Jean-Paul."

"Plot five, Commandant."

Another vibration, this time more pronounced. The ship was slowing down. The line showing the depth of the bottom was still climbing.

"Stop engines. Prepare to anchor."

Jean-Paul's reply was almost simultaneous with the voice of the first mate.

"Engines stopped."

"The anchor is cleared, Commandant."

For a few moments longer, the *Calypso* continued on her course. The bottom was now no more than fifteen feet beneath her keel, and the graph was recording a series of dark clouds just above it. They were schools of fish, directly beneath us. The atmosphere on the bridge was a trifle strained.

"Drop anchor!"

The sound of the anchor chain rattling through the hawse seemed to break the hpynotic spell which had claimed all of us. Suddenly, the air was filled with sound and conversation, lights were switched on, questions and answers were exchanged. When the engines stopped, the rest of the ship seemed to come alive, breathing a new, even more intense form of activity.

As I did on every such occasion, I had observed with an admiration tinged with pride as my father demonstrated yet again his perfect knowledge of the sea and of everything connected with it. I have known highly skilled seamen who make use of echo-sounding equipment as they would of a precise and impersonal instrument, but I feel sure that, to my father, it is something much more than this. He had guided us precisely to the spot we were searching for, with as much sureness as if he were actually walking on the sea floor, with no hesitation whatever, using the ship and the elements themselves as a virtuoso might use his favorite instrument. I could not help but think of it in these terms; a perfect and reassuring harmony. We were moored just at the edge of the plateau of coral, and while the anchor rested at a chain's length of about thirty feet, the prevailing current was such that the stern of the ship remained exactly above a depth of ninety to one hundred feet — the depths most propitious to our work.

On a map of East Africa, forty miles north-northwest of Djibouti, in the Gulf of Tadjoura, there is the shadowy area marked "Shab Arab Reef,"* but this is slightly redundant, since the word "Shab" means "reef" in Arabic. As is true of all such reefs lost in the high seas, Shab Arab is a refuge for marine life. It is not difficult, therefore, to understand that by protecting and nourishing the smaller species, the reefs become a sort of food warehouse for the hunters from the deep. In choosing Shab Arab as our anchorage, we hoped to find an abundance of all forms of life, and especially of sharks.

Now the motors were completely silent, all motion had ceased, and the entire crew gathered in the wardroom to hear my father define the goals of the next day's work. When he had concluded, I took on the task of translating his intentions into the language of cinematography and specifying each individual's role.

Arrival at a new location, particularly if it takes place at night, always arouses in me a childlike, impatient enthusiasm. The smooth black water against the hull trembles with feverish activity. From time to time a very small fish will leap desperately into the air, attempting to escape an invisible pursuer whose dorsal fin traces a momentary furrow in the water, straight and sharp as an arrow. At the fierce flick of a tail, tiny galaxies of luminescent particles are born and die in an instant, bearing witness to the life or death of some tiny animal. Sometimes, perhaps, a louder splash will cause me to lift my eyes from the water just below, but I can see nothing but a network of ever-shortening waves, coruscating in the luminous path of moonlight. At such times, I long for an understanding as inscrutable and all-seeing as that of the gods.

At four o'clock in the morning, we began setting up our first operation of this day's work. We wanted to make an underwater film of a shark attacking a fish hooked on a line. As a beginning to our experiments with sharks, we catch a great many fish for use as bait, and on many occasions our victims have come to us reduced to nothing more than the head, the rest of the body having been cleanly bitten off. There have been times when it was impossible to bring in even a single fish, and I have seen a small boat commanded by

*The site of the experiments mentioned on page 117.

The presence of the small-fry fish of the reef guarantees that large predators are about.

Paul Zuéna, our first mate and master fisherman, return to the *Calypso* bearing only the remains of fish mutilated by barracudas or sharks.

Therefore, in order to bring our present task to a successful conclusion, one of our small, flat-bottom aluminum boats was equipped with two cameras, hung over the stern and just below water level. Between these two film cameras, a television camera covering the same field was linked to a receiver in the boat. Thus, Michel Deloire could watch the action on the television screen a few feet away and start his film cameras at the exact moment of his choice. Since any system of propulsion on the aluminum boat would have made the whole experiment impossible, it was towed behind another boat equipped with a forty-horsepower Johnson outboard motor. The towline was maintained at a length sufficient to keep the photographic boat well clear of either the wake or the turbulence caused by the propeller of the tow boat. A silvery decoy, or "spoon," was trailed just within the range of the cameras, about ten to twelve feet behind the aluminum boat.

It was dawn when we put these two boats in the water, and two hours later we were ready to begin. The delay was caused by the necessity of adjusting the angle of filming on the cameras, and covering the forward part of the photographic boat with a canvas, in order to screen the light of the blazing sun and thus improve Michel's view of the television screen. The system for mounting the cameras on the stern of the photographic boat was conceived and made on board the *Calypso* by our chief mechanic, Roger Dufrêche, and we soon discovered that it worked perfectly — holding the cameras securely in place and transmitting no vibration.

In the first few minutes of fishing, Paul Zuéna experienced no difficulty in bringing on board more than a hundred pounds of fish, including a tuna, some barracuda, and several amberfish. Michel filmed the fish as they chased the decoy and bit into it, and then the struggle that took place before they were finally captured. When the first shark attacked, it was not at all in the manner we had looked for as a result of our other experiences in fishing for bait. A caranx weighing between sixteen and twenty pounds had been fighting the line for two or three minutes when Michel first saw the shark, following in the wake of the desperately battling fish. At almost the same moment as he appeared on the television screen, Paul saw the triangular fin break the surface just behind their boat. Michel's fingers were already gripping the trigger that would start the cameras, but the shark seemed in no hurry. He simply followed behind, effortlessly it seemed, and keeping a distance of exactly three feet

The smaller cage, on the right, was to prove that we had been overconfident in reckoning with the danger from small sharks, for the bars were not closely enough spaced to keep them out.

between himself and the caranx. It was only when Paul began to haul in our captive that the attack took place. The shark accelerated as swiftly as if he had been launched from a bow, seemed to pass the caranx without having touched it, momentarily blotted out the television screen and then vanished. The whole thing had been so sudden that, despite the tension of the moment, no one had reacted. Only the bleeding head Paul finally hauled into the boat attested to the reality of the attack. The caranx had bccn cut in two just behind the gills. The semicircle that marked its death was perfectly clean and sharp, and yet it had required no more than a fraction of a second for the shark to accomplish it.

All through that morning, Michel filmed attacks of varying kinds, sometimes slow and calculated, sometimes instant and terrifying. In one case, the

This is the type of encounter that really makes the day. It is rare to see a fish of that size. It is a grouper. His mouth open, he plans on devouring a fish that Serge had harpooned earlier for shark bait.

Serge, trying to retrieve the fish for his original shark-baiting purpose; we are not in the business of tagging groupers, and it would have been a wasted effort to forego the bait, but this grouper was so beautiful that we finally consented to let him have his dinner. The photograph was shot at one fiftieth of a second and the jaw of the fish is blurred. This demonstrates the incredible speed at which groupers project their mouths open, absorbing an extreme quantity of water, thus sucking in their prey.

His gills are opened wide to eject this tremendous amount of water, while his eye is rolled back by the effort. He has the fish completely in his mouth and he is about to withdraw.

Serge is still holding on. Having gained some ground, he has succeeded in liberating more of the fish. But the grouper did not submit, and the bait was still stuck inside the mouth of the gigantic fish.

shark had swallowed the entire fish and found himself caught on the same decoy his prey had swallowed. Obviously, however, the line was not strong enough for his weight and he broke it almost at once. At about noon, Michel, Paul, and their helpers returned to the *Calypso,* exhausted by the heat and nervous tension, but happy with the success of the mission. They also brought back enough fish to furnish bait for the dives we planned that afternoon.

As the objective of our first dive, we had planned that Serge would mark as many sharks as possible, and also spear a fish in the midst of the shark pack, so that we might observe the results. Serge was to occupy the big steel cage, while I would be in a small aluminum cage held on a horizontal level about six feet from the bottom by cast-iron weights made fast to lengths of rope. Two television cameras — one in each cage — would record the scene for my father and Doctor Eugenie Clark on the bridge of the *Calypso*. I carried two cameras, to film whatever happened around Serge and the big cage.

The water was the color of a translucent opal, so clear that I could make out the bottom, some seventy-five feet below, almost as soon as I entered. There were at least a dozen sharks cruising slowly back and forth along the length of the *Calypso's* red hull. They did not seem either very large or very aggressive, but their number foretold the possibility of some problems. Just above the level of the sand bottom, I could make out the forms of still other sharks, but it was difficult to estimate their size or number, since their grayish silhouettes were confused with the shadows they cast on the parallel ridges dug in the sand by the current. Seen from above, they were incredibly supple in their movements and seemed to be wandering aimlessly around the elongated silhouette of the *Calypso* projected on the bottom by the sun.

Serge's cage came gently to rest, raising a fine cloud of sand which dissipated almost at once. From where I lay watching, the environment of water made his movements seem as graceful as those of a dancer as he opened the door, slipped outside, and turned the cage around so that it was facing into the sunlight. Indifferent to the sharks, a large turtle paddled slowly toward the cage and proceeded to examine it at close hand, rather like a nearsighted old man. Serge offered it a piece of fish, which it ignored, and then it turned and swam away, with long, untroubled sweeps of its paddlelike front legs. For some reason, it reminded me of those old men who sit in the sun along the streets of Spanish villages and occasionally walk a few steps to visit with friends.

The sharks were becoming more and more numerous. There must have been at least fifty around us now, but they were still slow and indifferent in movement.

I had not noticed the arrival of an enormous grouper, which passed to my right and planted itself on the sand not more than three feet away from Serge. It was a bluish-black color, at least six feet long and seeming almost as big around. Its mouth opened and closed to the rhythm of its breathing. There was a terrible white scar across the top of its head, and one pectoral fin had been almost completely torn away. The grouper is a fish of rather terrifying appearance, giving an impression of brutal strength. Its alert little eyes seem extremely wary, and I know that it is capable of starting to move with incredible rapidity. Serge tossed it the piece of fish the turtle had refused. It drifted onto the sand a foot or so in front of the grouper, which simply opened its mouth a trifle wider, but made no other movement. The piece of fish disappeared, sucked in by the displacement of water. It was a fascinating spectacle, so fascinating indeed that I forgot about the sharks, although they were beginning to grow a trifle restless. With each tidbit Serge tossed to it, the enormous fish inhaled a little water and the morsel of our bait seemed to fly into its mouth, where it was instantly swallowed up. (Later on, I was to remember this moment, when Canoë and I found ourselves face to face with a fish of the same species but twice as large.) As a final offering, Serge flung out a barracuda weighing twenty pounds. It was absorbed as swiftly and easily as the other, smaller pieces, and then the grouper bestirred itself and swam away, as indifferently as it had arrived.

The sharks were now passing back and forth between our cages, almost with familiarity, seeming only slightly more nervous, a trifle more swift. Serge began scattering little crumbs of fish, so that their scent would permeate the water and attract our targets within reach of his marking spear. The circle began to close in immediately and the usual carrousel began. Sharks were arriving from every side, and I had the impression that there must be hundreds of them. They were of all sizes, ranging from quite small to more than six feet, and at least four different species were represented. In the space of the nine feet or so that separated our cages, I counted seven at one moment. They practically blocked my view of Serge. They swept by rapidly and sometimes turned on their own tails to snatch at a few crumbs of fish. Serge's spear was kept constantly in action, planting the little banderillas next to the dorsal fin,

Having abandoned the fish to the grouper, Serge proceeds to bait sharks with a barracuda caught that morning.

The frenzy starts when all those fish crumbs begin to surround the cages. The scent from them agitates the sharks' nerves.

Serge successfully tags a shark that is snapping at the barracuda he is holding in his left hand.

Another successful tagging.

and the general excitement grew to such a point that I saw one shark hurl himself in pursuit of another and tear away the little orange plaque with which he had been marked.

The sea itself seemed to have gone mad, filled with hurtling forms crossing each other's paths in meaningless, disordered trajectories. I retreated to the farthest corner of my cage, since it was open at the front and I could not close it. Serge tossed out the head of a caranx as large as a football, and the frenzy surrounding us reached a fever pitch. Ten sharks came down on it at once, and then attacked each other ferociously in the attempt to gain possession of the prize. In order to film this, I had to lift my head and shoulders out of the cage, and a shark managed to squeeze himself halfway in. I dropped the camera and used both hands to force him back through the bars. In doing so, I got several cuts on my fingers from the rough skin along his jaw, but fortunately for me he did not close it on them. Profiting from an instant of relative calm, I recovered the camera, but just as I was drawing back into the cage another shark smashed the reflector on its light attachment.

The situation now was becoming untenable. They were biting furiously at everything and shaking their heads in a kind of demented fury as they fought among themselves to tear apart whatever morsel of fish they had obtained. One shark succeeded in getting into Serge's cage, and Serge was forced to beat him off with the point of his marking spear. In the meantime, another had found and snatched up the whole sack of fish in the cage. He fled at once, followed by all the rest of the pack. In a sense, it was a stroke of luck for us, since the period of calm that followed gave us time to regain our composure and set things to right in our cages. The water was cloudy now and visibility had greatly decreased. I glanced at the counter on my camera, to be sure that I still had sufficient film, and decided to continue. The light was still functioning and I managed to get the reflector back into something resembling its original shape. At the same time, Serge was busily repairing his twisted marking spear.

When he had finished, he glanced over at me, and when he saw me nod, he took the spear gun from its bracket in the cage and fired a spear into a small shark, piercing its body from one side to the other. I prepared myself for a rush from all the rest of the pack, but it was exactly the reverse that occurred. The movement of all the other sharks immediately became more deliberate, and they withdrew to some distance from the cages. I was really taken completely by surprise. After having heard so many stories concerning cannibalism in sharks, this sudden timidity and mistrust confused me. One might actually have thought they now realized we were dangerous and were keeping their distance. Serge pulled sharply on his line to withdraw the spear, and the wounded shark swam off, trailing a cloud of blood. The others moved out of his path, but they nonetheless followed him discreetly. Perhaps they were waiting until he was farther from the source of danger before devouring him — I don't know — but I did notice that, as soon as he had disappeared, the sharks remaining in the area were again on the alert and the carrousel started up again.

This time, rather than aiming at another shark, Serge speared a red snapper. He was a large, strong fish and his desperate battle for survival brought on a renewal of the frenzy of a few moments earlier. In one violent leap, the unfortunate snapper freed himself from the spear, but at the same moment a shark tore away a portion of his back. In his dying flight, he some-how swam between the bars of my cage and I clung to its sides with all my strength, attempting to beat off his enraged pursuers. I could feel the cage resounding, seeming to crack into pieces around me beneath the sledge-hammer blows of these maddened animals. At last, the snapper found a way out — and was instantly devoured. The water surrounding me was filled with twisting, tearing bodies, insensate with fury and almost hidden in trails of a dark-green blood. I thought of my father, hunched over the television screens above, watching this maniacal battle.

Jacques-Yves Cousteau's narrative

It was, in fact, because of the television equipment (two cameras below, one in each cage, and two closed-circuit receivers in the *Calypso's* chart room) that we on board were enabled to follow everything that happened to Philippe and Serge, or to Canoë and José Ruiz. It was a very popular program . . . The mechanics, the cook, the doctor, the crewmen — everyone invaded the bridge and clustered behind me, staring wide-eyed at the two screens which brought us simultaneous images of two aspects of the same occurrence. When I glanced behind me, I could see the gleam in the eyes of my companions and evaluate, from the tension reflected here, the fascination sharks hold for men. This electric atmosphere, which is inevitably created around the television screens when we are diving in a shark-infested area, is exactly the same as the atmos-

Now one shark has successfully retrieved the barracuda from Serge's grip, tearing it apart, while another is aggressively rushing to get a piece of the action.

A sliver of fish floating toward the cameraman's cage as a shark shoots for it like a torpedo. A diver is looking on in the background. In the upper-left corner, other sharks have also spotted this piece of fish and they, too, are rushing for it.

Serge has speared an innocent little fish that had passed by to witness the action. The sharks' reaction is instantaneous, as they make their dash for the poor fish.

Sharks have begun showing their excitement, shooting between the cages, four and five at a time, rushing past us in frustration, with quick nervous turns, biting at anything they find.

phere that fills a bull ring at the moment of truth. No other undersea adventure or experiment would release so much pent-up feeling in the members of our crew, and they have been dealing with sharks for more than fifteen years.

For me, television screens are an incomparable tool of observation. Pen clutched in hand, I am totally absorbed in these two jerky, glittering pictures, from beginning to end of each descent of the cages; hoping to note down the smallest point which might permit us to understand a little more of the motives of shark behavior. The undersea cameraman is provided with a radiotelephone, and so am I. I remain in constant communication with the team in the cages. Messages go through quite clearly from the surface to the bottom, but from the cages to the surface they are often quite difficult to understand. The diver's speech becomes nasal because of the increase in density of the air breathed in at a depth of sixty or seventy feet, and also because the sound of air bubbles escaping from the breathing apparatus obscures some words. I have, in fact, recommended that no conversation be carried on unless it was necessary to ask for a change in the placement of the cages or to interrupt the operation for reasons of safety.

Each time the cages are brought back to the ship, the divers come to me and share their personal observations. It is these men, the direct witnesses to what has taken place, who are the most sensitive element in all our experiments. It is they who, in *living* these experiments, are at the very sources of the information we are seeking. They may remark an entire sequence of indices which sometimes seem of no significance, but which I carefully note down. Undersea television is totally incapable of replacing direct human observation, but through it I am assured of constant contact with the various teams, as they replace each other in the water. And this, in turn, makes it possible for me to form a synthesis of the reports of all the divers.

Dives involving the use of the cages require lengthy preparation, and are difficult to set in operation. In the course of this expedition, we carried out a total of twenty-three such dives, averaging thirty-five minutes in length and anywhere between twenty-five and ninety feet in depth, at varying hours of both night and day. In the course of her stay on board the *Calypso,* Doctor Eugenie Clark often came into the chart room to watch the television screens with me and was essential in interpreting the events taking place below.

Shab Arab, which Philippe has described so graphically, is teeming with life. Netting more than two hundred pounds of fish (which we pass out to the sharks every day) is a formality requiring no more than half an hour. In addition to this, sharks themselves are extremely abundant in the vicinity of the reef, but since they cannot always be found, I have been led to the belief that they travel in bands, like wolves. Our numerous markings have, however, confirmed the fact that the sharks of Shab Arab are of a relatively sedentary nature. There are all sizes of them, some very large ones included, but the average size — which is a reflection of their average age — is smaller than that of the sharks to be found on the reefs in the Suakin region of the Red Sea. They became accustomed to our presence very rapidly, and seemed to have understood that we brought them food. Several times, we watched as they entered the divers' cages, and, each time, we on the surface were doubtless more frightened than the divers themselves; but on such occasions they never made any attempt to bite, only desperately trying to escape from the confined enclosure. Their period of excitement goes on for as long as there is food to be had. As soon as our sacks are empty, our sharks turn away and swim off into the distance. A large shark does not like the idea of a good piece of our fish being taken away by a smaller shark; he will race at him, seeming almost as though he were growling, bare his teeth and appear prepared for a kill, but he will not bite. The big nurse sharks will come and eat from the hand of the divers, but if they should be given a good fat piece of fish, one of the smaller white-finned sharks will approach and literally snatch it from their mouths. They would never dare do this sort of thing with a larger shark of their own species. They all prefer fresh fish to our refrigerated supplies, but they will grow sulky if the fish has been caught even so recently as the day before.

All these seemingly reassuring remarks have no significance whatever when one of the "frenzies" described by Philippe takes place. On such occasions, as we watch from the safety of the ship, we are overcome first by anxiety and then by terror. Twice, I have felt compelled to intervene and cut short the experiment by having the cages recalled to the surface.

Philippe Cousteau's narrative

I always remember the foregoing episode with surprise, since I had seen at least one case in which the outcome was very different: a wounded shark inspired not fear or caution but cannibalistic fury in the others. At a time when we were anchored near a reef in the Red Sea, we had decided to blast a passage

The sharks have now seized the fish.

It takes about five seconds for them to really take a bite and swallow it.

After that, their excitement is generated to the point of rushing on anything they can devour, and anything that happens to be in their path.

This one passing right in front of our camera is tagged. The small red tag following his dorsal fin floats like a little *banderilla* planted on his back on the near side. The tail of another shark underneath is moving by, much closer.

This photograph was shot with a very wide-angle lens, meaning that the sharks are as close as four feet — even closer — to the camera.

through the barrier with dynamite, so that our small boats might enter the lagoon. During the first tryouts of the electric detonators, Eugène Lagorio, who was in charge of setting up the necessary equipment, tossed one of them overboard, after having linked it with the plunger on the ship. He did this for two reasons: to avoid any possibility of someone's being hurt and to test the waterproof qualities of the detonator itself. At the precise moment at which Eugène pressed down on the plunger, a small shark none of us had seen swallowed the detonator. He had probably been attracted to it by its casing of brilliant copper. Before any of us had had a chance to move, we heard a muted detonation and then watched as the little shark began to sink to the bottom, trailing blood. Almost immediately, a large *Albimarginatus* appeared from out of nowhere, lunged at our unfortunate victim and sliced him in two with a single movement of his jaw. Then he turned on himself, swallowed the remainder of the little shark and went on his way, his belly swollen with food. Once again, we had been given a demonstration of the irregularity of the reactions of sharks. Their attitude is probably a function of circumstances which our atrophied senses cannot detect.

In this context, one other matter comes to mind; a fact related to the personality of sharks — because they do have a personality, despite their primitive appearance. In the first stages of a dive in a new territory, it is simple to mark a certain number of sharks almost immediately. But then we notice that all those that present themselves for our food have already been marked. In a short time, the divers are surrounded with sharks bearing a little banderilla, and it becomes impossible to learn anything about those that continue to remain aside. This is not a question of species, since the same thing occurs with all species. The only explanation that seems reasonable to me is that some sharks are more courageous than others of like size and species. This discovery had considerable importance in my mind, since it led me to observe

This is a shot of the same area, recounting the same type of frenzy much later at night. It is even more strange and frightening in the dark.

The bait in the upper-left-hand corner is being sought by two sharks, which are fighting for it as a herd of others are desperately trying to find the food by sense of smell. Since fish-bait scent permeates the area (we started distributing it two hours earlier), they are not very definite as to its location.

A typical daytime frenzy. An incredible disarray of twisting and turning bodies, tearing at the same piece of fish.

Finally, one shark snatches the food and absconds, pursued by all the others.

The chaos is now compounded. That shark exiting from Serge's cage had entered it by bending the cage bars out of shape on the other side. Serge is now pushing him out. We were very lucky that no harm befell any of us.

and marvel at the life of sharks, rather than regarding them simply as beautiful but potentially dangerous objects.

Since these earlier experiences, it has become possible for us — at least, in the majority of cases — to estimate the atmosphere of a dive in an area of sharks. From the moment of entrance into the water, we could foresee the probable tempo of the *corrida* and decide the need for strong protection or none at all. The trap, however, lies in trusting too much in this sense of perception, since, as we have observed so many times, the reactions of sharks are always unpredictable and often seem to reach the point of folly.

On the same evening as the great frenzy at Shab Arab, we decided to carry out a night dive. This time, we set the cages one above the other, instead of side by side. In this manner, the diver filming the experiment was situated above and could obtain a close-up view of the entire operation.

The instant the lower of the two cages had touched water, a pack of sharks struck at it as if they had been propelled by rockets. They tore at the steel of the bars, bit through the electric cables, and demolished several waterproof lights. The flat-bottomed aluminum boat, returning alongside after an exploratory trip, was violently attacked by sharks attempting to bite into the propeller of the outboard motor. But this larger and more powerful dentist's drill must have cut through several jaws, since blood began to spread in great, swirling clouds. The sharks, however, succeeded in stalling the forty-horsepower motor and breaking the cotter pin on the propeller. Canoë, wisely, ordered the cages brought up immediately, and the experiment was put off until another day.

On the next morning, there was only a single, small shark near the ship, and no others came throughout the day. What mysterious reason had caused them to flee we will know only when we have learned how to analyze the infinity of pressure waves, the new scents and sounds, those secret messengers of the sea.

We had recorded some interesting encounters with sharks during our Conshelf Two experience in the Red Sea, and we now turn to these for the light they throw on shark behavior.

TEN:

Sharks and Settlers
**The Story of Conshelf Two
and the sharks.
In the saucer we meet the
Abyssal Shark.
The settlers.**

Philippe Cousteau's narrative continues

I tightened the slipknot around my father's ankles, tapped lightly on his shoulder, and took my position six feet behind him, putting a little tension in the rope. He yanked his legs and I felt a tug on the rope; it was the "go" signal. At the same instant I heard the hushed noise of the camera starting to run. I began swimming straight ahead, slowly increasing speed until I reached the maximum I could do. Glancing rapidly above my shoulder, I could see the brilliantly lit twin windows right behind me, and clearly defined on them the silhouette of my father, whom I was towing backward straight out into the night. The dark water was warm and full of phosphorescent particles streaking the obscurity like innumerable shooting stars. I was breathing fast and hard, swimming as rapidly as I could, and when I glanced back again, the windows of the undersea house were far behind. Yet, I could still see shapes moving across the lighted frames. I felt another tug on my line and stopped, beads of sweat running down my forehead and along my nose behind the face plate. Turning around, I quickly freed my father's legs from the rope and we started back toward the Conshelf Two village.

From a distance, at night, the station looked like a science-fiction outerspace base. Multicolored rotating beacons marked the shape of the saucer hangar on the right, of the big "Starfish" main station in the center with the

This is a typical Red Sea or Indian Ocean reef, falling straight from the surface as far down as 2600 feet. The diver is using a low ledge for protection against a pack of sharks that were right in front of him. These cliffs of coral growth are an awesome sight.

Some moments in the water prove poetic and magnificent, devoid of all false excitement, and filled with joy and beauty. This is the crevice between rocks and coral heads where the diver delights in swimming between the rocks and on into the overhang.

two picture windows, and farther below, of the deep cabin. Scattered around were several shacks, which housed equipment for everyday work. The upper station was resting on a sandy ledge thirty-six feet below the surface against the coral wall of the outer reef of the Shab Rumi (Roman Reef) atoll in the southern Red Sea. Fifty feet below the main-station level was the deep cabin, which was hung along the vertical coral cliff that formed the base of the whole reef. Up above our heads the elongated shape of the *Calypso's* hull reflected the green and red flashes of the beacons. We hurried back to the safety of the main habitat.

The Conshelf Two experiment had been planned to demonstrate the feasibility of manned undersea stations. The year was 1963. The location had been chosen so as to be away from all our bases of supplies and because of the extreme weather conditions. If it succeeded there on the desolate coast of Sudan, it would be possible to achieve the same thing anywhere on the globe. A team of six divers lived in the main station for a month, and two oceanauts occupied the deep cabin for two weeks. Chosen from professional and nonprofessional divers, the team experimented with new gas mixtures and worked all day at underwater chores. In the main habitat, "Starfish House," a complete biology laboratory supervised by Professor Vaissière studied reef ecology as well as microorganisms. One of the studies conducted during the Conshelf Two adventure was the intereffect of a human colony and its natural undersea surroundings.

During the experiment, everything had been recorded on film, and a movie entitled *World Without Sun* was made from the footage. It was for the purpose of shooting one of the sequences of this film that my father and I had been in the water that night. It was a long pullback from close to the habitat windows, and far into the darkness. My father held the camera and I pulled him backward for a distance of about a hundred yards. The result was such an unreal effect that many people believed, when seeing the shot on screen, that it had been faked in a studio. It had not been faked, and I remember my feelings as I swam in total darkness in waters where, as my father will recount, many sharks were lurking.

In fact, these four weeks of work on the bottom of the sea helped us to realize better what the relationship between future undersea settlers and their environment will be when man decides to colonize the sea floor. Understandably, we were most concerned with the problem of "sharks versus settlers."

Jacques-Yves Cousteau's narrative

The problem of sharks had been a major factor in all our preparations, and as is always the case when it comes to sharks, nothing had turned out as foreseen. At Shab Rumi, sharks were one of the favorite topics of conversation on board the two ships as well as in the houses beneath the sea.

"What has happened to all the sharks at Shab Rumi?" Albert (Bébert) Falco asked during one of our undersea dinners in Starfish House. "I explored the reefs along the Sudanese coast for more than eighty miles, and I found sharks everywhere; particularly here, at Shab Rumi. I hesitated to advise this location for the experiment, just because of them. And during the first weeks of work, when we were just setting up the village, they worried us constantly. What has happened to them now?"

"They are still here, Bébert," I said. "You saw some yourself, yesterday, at South Point. Kientzy reports having seen them every time he makes a dive from the Deep Cabin. And when I stand in the launch on the surface and there is a night dive going on down there, I am always worried, because I can see their fins, just a couple of hundred feet from the diver's lights."

"It's the same story with all the shark fisheries," Dumas remarked. "Everyone who thought he was going to make a fortune catching sharks, whether it was in South Africa or Australia, in the Gulf of Tadjoura or at Dakar, has eventually been forced to give it up. They may have a few months of miraculous catches, but then they find the sharks have gone. The same thing happened at Djibouti. In 1930 it was infested with sharks, but once the development of the port began, they went somewhere else. . . ."

I had personally met the most famous shark hunters, Captain Young, who wrote a classic book on sharks, and two remarkable women, Anita Conti and her associate, Paquerette, who had organized and directed a large shark fishery in Conakry. They all were of the opinion that sharks were smart enough to emigrate from fishing areas.

Here at Shab Rumi, however, since the first stages of our operations, we had disturbed the natural life of the reef as little as possible. I had forbidden

This is a mere example of the beauties of the reef, with its fan-coral background. The incredible shapes and colors of the fishes do not always seem to have a functional reason for being.

underwater spearfishing, and even fishing from the surface had been almost completely avoided. When we needed fish, we sent our small boats to hunt for them at a distance of more than five miles from our reef. We often distributed food to the moray eels, the snappers, the triggerfish, even to the barracudas. The moray eels came and ate from our hands. The triggerfish laid their eggs at the very doors of our undersea houses. One of them had actually been tamed by our diver-cook, Pierre Guilbert. In spite of our comings and goings, the savage bumpfish continued to sleep every night in the crevices no more than thirty feet from our village. We had even been adopted by an enormous barracuda we named Jules. We had hoped that the sharks, too, would remain, and we were equipped to study their habits without risk to ourselves or danger to them.

But they remained impervious to our lures. The live fish stocked in the fragile plastic enclosure constituted a form of provocation for them, but it had no effect. They had chosen to remain at a distance. Oh, we knew they were not very far away; they had simply enlarged the circumference of their circle around our installations. They came into the area only furtively, and at night.

A quarter of a mile or so from our village, at the southernmost tip of the atoll of Shab Rumi, there were still many open-ocean fish and sharks. One of these, a large tiger shark, was an old inhabitant of the region. He acted like a very sedentary Shab Rumi citizen. He circled around us every time we made an exploratory dive in those waters. (Philippe has told earlier how this brute hesitated for days before swallowing a spoiled carcass of beef that we had sunk right in the middle of his territory.)

In the third week of the Conshelf Two experiment, we wanted to collect geological samples from the reef at various depths. The oceanauts from Starfish House were in charge of gathering such samples in their authorized diving range, from thirty of eighty-five feet of depth. But deeper, such activity had not been planned for the two "black-mask oceanauts" living in the deep cabin. Accordingly, I organized a geological dive from the surface. Armand Davso was equipped with hammer and chisel. I took an underwater camera to film the action and Philippe accompanied us, carrying two spare cameras. We submerged. We rarely had gone down so fast as we did in trying to keep up with Davso, who was drawn down like a piece of lead by his sledge-hammer. We passed swiftly along Starfish House on the left, then along the deep cabin on the right. At one hundred and fifty feet, the vertical coral cliff ended abruptly and a grayish sandy beach sloped down to the "second cliff" a hundred feet away. There, on the edge of the new drop-off, stood one of our five small antishark cages, a shelter for oceanauts, connected to the undersea headquarters of Starfish House by special alarm signals. We had carefully installed and tested all this shark-proof emergency equipment, but had never had an opportunity to use it.

We sank deeper, reached 230 feet, stopped. I selected a big block of coral rock and triggered my camera; Davso started hammering heavily on the block. The loud, muffled clangs disrupted the silence of the deep. Almost at once, I saw in the field of my camera two large white-tip sharks emerging from the blue and rushing to the scene, straight toward Davso's back. I shouted in my mouthpiece. Davso did not hear and kept on hammering. Philippe then acted as a bodyguard and swam directly at them. They slowly altered their course, passed alongside Davso, circled close around us for a while, and vanished as they had come. We had had no time to retreat to the shark cage. . . . The loud hammering had attracted sharks as explosions do, and Philippe's decisive attitude had discouraged them.

We went back with the desired samples, watching the ponderous Davso climb the cliffs as a mountain climber would. Back on board, we told Davso the experience he had missed by being so conscientious in his work.

It does seem probable that sharks remain away from any center of human activity in the sea, more or less as tigers remain at a distance from the towns and villages of India. Inhabited undersea stations, which are certain to multiply in number in the future, will therefore have little to fear from sharks. But why should sharks withdraw thus, when they have had no experience with man, that newcomer to the ocean? I cannot help but relate this fact to observations we have often made on the high seas — primarily of scores of formidable deep-sea sharks remaining at a respectful distance from schools of dolphins or whales. It is possible that sharks vaguely identify us with these marine mammals. In that event, they would not hesitate to attack us if we were alone or in difficulty, but they will remain at a prudent distance from any of our collective installations.

It was now nine o'clock in the evening — time to call an end to our exchange of views on the subject of sharks, to take leave of our hosts, the oceanauts, to leave Starfish House, and to return to the *Calypso*. Dumas, Falco, and I got into our diving gear in the ready room. I suggested to my two comrades that we might make a short tour of the undersea village before going back to the surface.

The water slapped back and forth in the entrance hatch just as it would

The shark cages had been lowered out at sea. A tiger shark of considerable size is passing by. This is a fairly rare species. We consider tiger sharks extremely dangerous. Although we haven't had much experience with them, they are capable of grave damage. Their jaws are massive, teeth razor-sharp, muscles powerful, and their mouth is out of proportion to the size of their bodies.

in a very small swimming pool. One after the other, we slipped down through this horizontal doorway and found ourselves floating free in the darkness of night, behind the steel bars of the antishark vestibule. We lit our waterproof guide lights and left this big cage, which now appeared to have been a useless protection, since the sharks had left the area.

At first, we swam slowly over to the saucer hangar, and I lifted my head out of water in the interior of this strange garage beneath the sea. Our little submarine was there. A red light on the electric panel indicated that the batteries were being charged. After a brief look around, we returned to open water. The coral shelf dropped away sheer beneath us, and a moment or two later we could make out the vertical cylinder of the deep cabin. When we reached it, eighty-five feet beneath the surface, I glanced through the portholes. Kientzy and Portelatine had turned out all the lights and were doubtless seeking a period of sleep made difficult by the heat and humidity inside.

I hesitated to go down farther. At this time of night, the narrow beam of our lights was of little help, and the black void beneath us was a realm of fear. We pushed on to the base of the cliff and then swam along its embankment, one hundred and fifty feet below the surface. We came to a clump of black coral where, standing before us like some giant lobster trap, was our antishark cage Number One. It seemed to me that I had caught a glimpse of a long silhouette and the glittering reflection of a greenish eye. We turned and began the ascent of the cliffside. A swarm of brightly colored fish hovered around our four cubic enclosures as we passed. We could make out a dim light above us and a little farther out. That would be the *Calypso*. Beneath her stern, near the ladder we would use to climb aboard, hung a thirty-foot length of rope, weighted down with iron. In order to effect the indispensable breathing period that would protect us from accidents of decompression, we were forced to remain here for forty minutes, clinging to the rope in the darkness, accompanied rather disturbingly by our barracuda, Jules.

The *Calypso* was anchored just southwest of the island of Socotra, in the northern part of the Indian Ocean near the Gulf of Aden, where the bottom is about three hundred feet in depth. Henri Plé, who was on duty on the bridge, came to tell me that the saucer was ready. In spite of the overpowering heat, I pulled on a wool slipover: it would be cold below. The saucer was resting on its cradle on the afterdeck. Albert Falco and I weighed ourselves on a bathroom scale, and our respective weights were inscribed in chalk on a small blackboard. Armand Davso calculated the total and decided to add a little more water to the ballast inside the saucer. This correction should insure, roughly at least, the equilibrium of the little submarine.

Falco and I squeezed into the saucer, and as he carefully closed and screwed down the hatch, I regulated the oxygen supply, opened the ventilator of the air-purification system, checked the batteries, the oil pressure, and the heading indicated on the gyroscopic compass. I synchronized our timepieces and Falco turned on the tape recorder. He then signaled by telephone to Jacques Roux, the saucer's maintenance engineer, that everything was in working order. We stretched out on our stomachs on the foam-rubber mattresses, which had been designed so that our heads would be close to individual viewing portholes. Inside the saucer, there was a quiet but resonant ambiance resembling that of a factory. Some of the engines turned constantly, others started and stopped automatically, and contact elements snapped periodically. Maurice Léandri maneuvered the hydraulic crane that lifted the saucer from its cradle on the *Calypso's* deck, and for a few seconds we swung gently in the air. Then, with Maurice's habitual mastery of this operation, the saucer slipped gently into the sea, creating no more sound than the crumpling of a piece of silk.

Almost at once I saw two sharks cruising at some distance from us. Christian Bonnici, the diver in charge of getting the saucer safely away, did not lose sight of them for a moment, even though he was also carrying out his routine tasks. First, he scrubbed off the plexiglass portholes, and then, at a signal from Falco, climbed to the upper surface of the saucer, disconnected the telephone, and unhooked the last nylon rope linking us with the world outside. Slowly, the saucer began to go down. Our echo sounder clearly indicated the edge of the reef, three hundred feet below. We settled on it just a few minutes later. It was a grayish plain consisting of mud and fragments of stone. Falco dropped the seventy-five-pound outside ballast, which had helped to carry us down, and regulated our ability to descend or ascend by pumping out several liters of water. Next, he switched on our primary motive power, twin pusher jets, coughing out powerful streams of water to our stern, and we headed to the south, along the line of sharpest descent.

At a depth of 325 feet, we reached the sharply defined line that separated the plateau from the cliff. And here, as in the Red Sea, we came across an overhanging "sidewalk" that ran along the upper edge of the cliff. Until this time, no instrument, no echo sounder, however precise, had ever detected the presence of this ledge. It is a perfectly horizontal *corniche,* from six to

The beam of our lamps detects a blue shark swimming close by, his mouth open for breathing, and his wide eyes adapted for night vision. His reflection on the flat, calm surface appears almost as worrisome and perilous as he actually is.

thirty feet wide, running continuously along the crests of the ridges, through all the reefs, the islands, and the buried volcanic peaks — always at a depth of 330 to 350 feet. This discovery, which we could have made only from the saucer, suggests that the surface of the sea in this area was at this level during one of the great glacial epochs thousands of years ago.

The two sharks had followed us as far as this, but they deserted us when we began drifting slowly down along the cliff. On this wall of naked rock, life forms became progressively rare. Occasionally we would sight some gorgonians, which are also known as fan coral, some Bryozoa and small crustaceans, but very few fish of any kind.

At about 450 feet, the saucer stopped sinking and came to rest between two levels of water, as if it were poised on a sea floor. "It's the thermocline," Falco said. We had reached the frontier between the warm surface water and the cold water of the depths, and were floating on a layer of fluid that was denser because it was colder. We could have continued our descent at once by letting a few quarts of water into our internal ballast, but we preferred to let nature make the necessary correction herself, by chilling the outer shell of the saucer. The thermometer fell from 32° to 25° Centigrade. Falco put on a sweater. In a few moments, our gravitational descent resumed.

At a depth of more than 850 feet, we reached the end of the vertical desert. The cliff here was riddled with large crevices, teeming with fat red fish weighing as much as five or six pounds, and also some large groupers. We settled on a kind of step about thirty feet wide and paused to examine the animated world around us. The rocks were studded with strange little crustaceans, eight inches long and waving claws almost as large as themselves; the cliff walls were almost hidden by clouds of shrimp. Fish we had never seen before were emerging from holes everywhere, as if they were eager to inspect us: some of them were bright red, while others were a motley design of mauve and yellow; still others were marked with vertical stripes of brown and white. As far as the eye could see across the mud and pebbly-sand expanse of the flat bottom, there were thousands, millions of crabs.

We started the jets again, heading east and skirting the base of the cliff. Everywhere we looked, the ground was masked by a tide of tangled, marching, kicking crabs, most of them about the size of a man's fist. This gigantic congress of crabs must certainly have been brought about by the fact that it was their mating time. Falco and I spent almost an hour gliding over this living carpet, occasionally pausing for a few moments to observe the behavior of the crabs.

Suddenly, Falco cried out, "Look, Commandant, to your left, in the distance!" I squinted my eyes against the porthole, trying to see as far as possible. A form that was still not clear to me was climbing slowly toward us. It was a shark, but an enormous, unbelievable shark. He was swimming straight toward the saucer, as though he were blinded by our lights. I did not at first recognize the species; it was the monster's size that impressed me most. He must have been twice as long as our little submarine, and weighed easily three thousand pounds. He swept around the saucer in a majestic arc and miscalculated his course; a powerful sweep of his tail shook us up considerably. Obviously, we were in no danger inside our steel armor, but it is a rather strange experience to feel yourself being knocked about by a creature of this size, almost nine hundred feet below the surface of the sea.

The enormous beast made several turns in front of us, while still caught in the glare of our lights. I could not help but admire his power and grace — the strength of a bull, the supple movement of a serpent. He had six branchial clefts on either side of his head, and this helped me to identify him. He was a *Hexanchus griseus,* sometimes called a cow shark. He is very rarely encountered, presumably because he inhabits areas of great depth and comes to the surface only on very rare occasions. The way our giant "six-clefts" friend behaved, I could not help but associate him with two other giants, even larger than he, the whale shark and the basking shark. They all make only rare or seasonal appearances at the surface. The rest of the time they vanish to untold depths and provinces; practically nothing is known of their lives in the depths. Maybe some of them are responsible for these mysterious large excavations in the mud that we have often photographed with automatic deep cameras lowered to the bottom of the Mediterranean, eight thousand feet down.

Our cow shark swam around us long enough for us to film him, and then bumped into the saucer again, apparently by accident. In any event, he was suddenly seized with panic, gave another violent flick of his tail, and disappeared into the depths of his own kingdom. And this kingdom, alas, was still inaccessible to the diving saucer. Poised at the edge of the second cliff, Falco and I swept the void into which the giant had disappeared with the saucer's headlights, hoping to attract him back toward us. After half an hour

Blue shark in the night.

of waiting in vain, Falco jettisoned a fifty-five-pound ballast weight, so that we could return to the surface. Twenty minutes later, we were picked out of the water by the *Calypso*. For many weeks after that, both Falco and I talked and dreamed of the extraordinary dive and of our meeting with the cow shark, the lord of depths that are still beyond our reach.

Coexistence between sharks and settlers is not always entirely peaceful. We had a dramatic demonstration of this near the reef of Shab Arab, in the Gulf of Aden. The *Calypso* was anchored at the extreme northern edge of the reef, above an area of vertical cliffs, which, here too, dropped straight down to a depth of nearly nine hundred feet.

Falco and I decided to make a night dive along these cliffs in the diving saucer. As soon as it had been put in the water, we saw several large sharks in the beams from our headlights. Their number increased rapidly as we went down, and in a short time we estimated that there were at least three dozen of them surrounding us. They seemed much more active than was normal. We set down the saucer on a little mud slope at a depth of about 350 feet, to carry out the usual instrument check and adjust our buoyancy before continuing our exploration. Through the portholes, perfectly safe inside our metal shell, we could see all those sinister silhouettes, now circling very close around us. The spectacle was unique and magnificent. Unfortunately, the saucer's cameras were able to film only a very small part of the mad round dance. We decided to return to the surface and set up a dive with an anti-shark cage, so that our cinematographer could film our divers and this exceptional horde of sharks at the same time.

Half an hour later, after we had attached powerful floodlights to the cage, it was put into the water, empty, as usual, and dropped to a depth of one hundred feet. The cameraman, Pierre Goupil, his assistant, Pierre Duhalde, and two divers, Christian Bonnici and Raymond Coll, followed it into the water, carrying their cameras and shark billies. The brilliantly lit cage provided them with a perfect point of reference, and they went down rapidly, experiencing no particular fear. When they were halfway to the cage, they could see the green glitter of the eyes of a dozen or so sharks reflected in the beam from their own flood lamps. They set to work calmly to film them, but the pack of sharks at once began circling around our crew, and as the circles drew tighter the number of sharks increased. Within a few moments, there were about seventy of them in the immediate vicinity. Suddenly the divers realized that there was no longer a question of filming but of self-protection.

Goupil was confronted with a difficult decision. The antishark cage could hold only three men, which would leave the fourth alone and at the mercy of the vast pack of predators. Goupil rang several times on the alarm, to have the cage pulled back to the *Calypso's* deck, and then seized his assistant, who was the least experienced of the divers, and pushed him inside. Then Goupil, Bonnici, and Coll installed themselves as well as they could on top of the cage, sitting back to back and facing out toward every possible angle of attack.

The sharks immediately broke their circling formation and launched themselves forward like wolves, directly toward the men, obviously aware of their crushing superiority in numbers. The divers fought back with shark billies, cameras, lights, anything they had in their hands. On the deck of the *Calypso,* no one had yet grasped the gravity of the situation. Following Goupil's signal, one of the divers who was operating the winch thought it best to bring up the cage very slowly, to facilitate the process of decompression for the men below. The closer it came to the surface, the more fiercely the sharks attacked, but somehow the three men on top of the cage managed to beat them off. When it broke water at last and was hauled aboard, they were all unhurt. The frustrated killers thrashed the surface into a miniature storm.

Goupil had scarcely recovered from the shock of this attack when he suggested going down again, but with just two men, this time locked inside the cage before it was lowered into the water. Since the diving saucer would be in no danger, he wanted to film it with this horde of sharks, rather than risk the lives of other divers. The idea seemed a good one, so we altered the floodlight arrays on the cage and Pierre Goupil and Daniel Tomasi took their places inside, where they, too, would be perfectly safe. Falco and I piloted the saucer to a depth of about eighty feet, in the midst of the shark pack. All this, of course, required a certain amount of time. When the saucer finally drew close to the cage, Falco and I were astonished by the sight of Goupil and Tomasi, having dropped their cameras, performing a crazy kind of dance inside the cage. They were leaping about in every direction possible and slapping constantly at their ankles. Thousands of little white dots were swirling around them, picked out clearly in the brilliant light of the projectors, and reminding us of mosquitoes or gnats caught in the lights of a garden on a summer night. The human silhouettes inside the cage were twisting into every imaginable shape, as if seized by some sudden madness. The cameras and the sharks had been forgotten. Neither Falco nor I could understand what had happened, but a moment later, we saw the cage start up toward the

This blue shark leaves the standard wake at the surface; he is about to pursue the large group of squid on the other side.

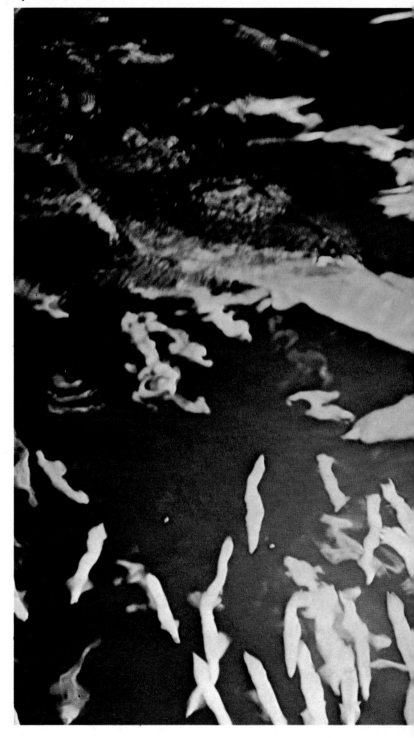

surface, doubtless as a result of the second sounding of the alarm that night.

Half an hour later the saucer was back in its cradle on the deck of the *Calypso,* and we climbed out. The after deck was deserted, but it was also covered with blood stains. I raced to the officers' mess and found Goupil and Tomasi stretched out on tables there, with bandages around their ankles and their features still drawn with lines of pain. There were spots of blood on the floor, on the tables, and even on the partitions. The doctor was per-plexed and anxious. Our friends had been attacked, as soon as they entered the water, by thousands of "sea mosquitoes," which are tiny isopods, a form of planktonic crustacean almost invisible to the eye but as ferocious for its size as the famous piranhas of the Amazon. The claws of these isopods tear off a minute portion of flesh every time they bite. Each of our two victims had lost at least a pint of blood.

Goupil and Tomasi had been completely protected against them by their neoprene diving suits — except for the small area of their ankles between the rubber fins and the bottom of the tight-fitting pants. As the cage was being hauled to the surface, they had been battling these mini-monsters and were almost unaware of the sharks encircling them. Maurice Léandri, who was oper-ating the crane, had stopped it for five minutes, while the cage was still several feet below the surface, to allow for the obligatory decompression period.

Goupil said to me: "During that halt, I was suffering such torture from the mosquitoes that I was tempted to open the door and go out and join the sharks. . . ."

When the *Calypso* came back to home port from the Conshelf Two experiment in the Red Sea, we had gained considerable experience with sharks and with manned undersea stations. We began thinking about the future of human settlements on the bottom of the oceans and about the relationship that would develop between sharks and settlers.

We started at once to prepare for Conshelf Three — twenty-seven days at 330 feet in the Mediterranean. The experiment was to take place two years later, but without delay we drafted long-term programs in the fields of en-gineering, of physiology, and of practical applications.

In Marseilles, facilities were built to carry tank dives to a theoretical depth of five thousand feet; in such chambers, it would be possible to deter-mine the reasonable limits of helium-oxygen "saturation dives," as well as to test the intricate instrumentation needed in the very deep Conshelf station of the future.

Plans were made for a three-hundred-ton, ten-man submarine completely self-supported and capable of becoming a mobile "home under the sea" for four oceanauts diving and working extensively at depths down to two thousand feet. This independent mobile settlement, called "l'Argyronète," is now under construction.

An international training center for scientist-oceanauts was proposed to UNESCO and recommended by the Intergovernmental Oceanographic Conference.

Projects were studied to carry the activity of undersea settlers into various fields such as undersea farming, mining, drilling for oil, oil exploitation, geological and biological observations and studies, and entertainment centers.

A long-range program was outlined to develop an amphibious man: *Homo aquaticus.*

The future of human settlements on and beyond the continental shelf is almost unlimited. Of course, I do not believe that human colonies will ever emigrate to the sea floor forever: we are too much dependent on our natural environment, and there would be no serious reason to abandon all those things we love: sunshine, fresh air, country, landscapes . . .

But there will be, more and more, important tasks in science and industry that will require temporary but extended settlements of large groups of human beings working on the bottom of the sea for several months at a time. Locked there by decompression problems, they will need medical and recreational facilities, very much in the same way as oil specialists settle in the desert for periods of — say — five months. These requirements mean huge constructions and investments. Such schemes will be possible only when a quantity of problems are solved. Among these problems is protection against sharks.

Today we think that sharks retreat from an area where settlements are constructed. But we are sure that they do not retreat very far; they stay in the vicinity. They may be attracted back to the inhabited area by explosions or by a variety of noises like bangs or clangs. And we do not know if, after a longer period, they would not overcome their fear and come back in packs to attack isolated small groups of workers. A lot more research is necessary. A good working theory would be that the world of fish in general and of sharks in particular is less of a visual world than it is a world of acoustic and pressure waves. Sound and pressure waves of yet little-known frequencies may be able to attract sharks or to repel them from the settlements.

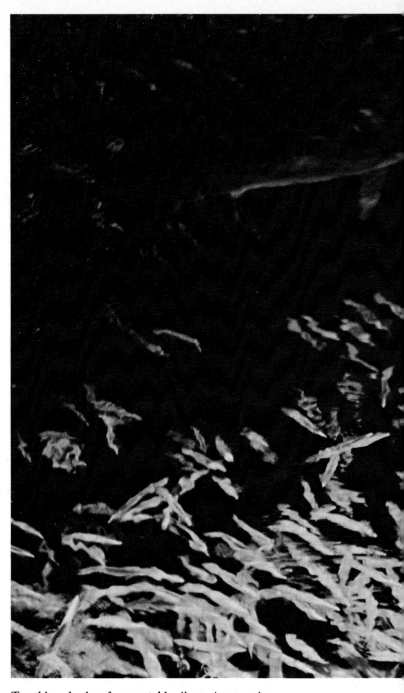

Two blue sharks of respectable dimensions, eating.

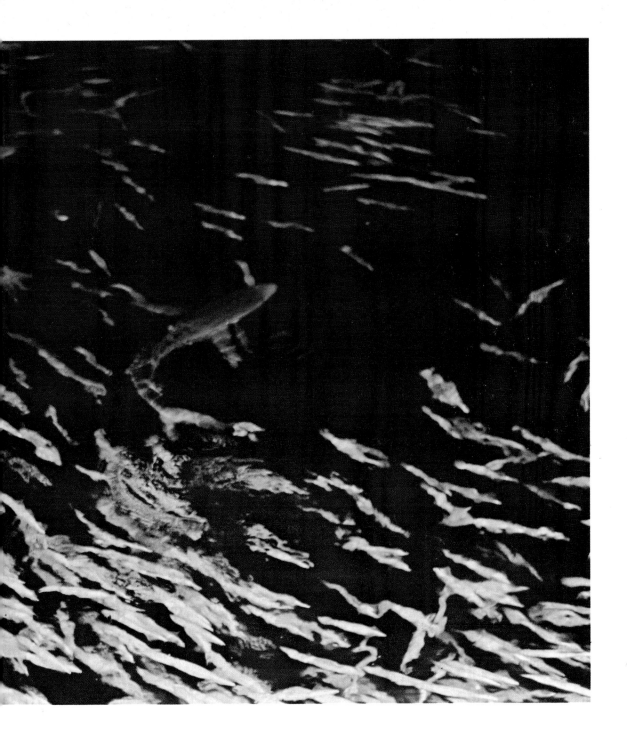

ELEVEN:
Peaceful Giant
Our encounter
with a whale shark.
Shark legends.

Philippe Cousteau's narrative

It was not until May of 1967 that we finally encountered a whale shark. For a week the *Calypso* had been sailing a north-northwest course in the Indian Ocean, from Diego-Suarez toward the Gulf of Tadjoura. The stopover in Diego-Suarez had been our first important port of call since February and, as it always was, our reception in this great port of the Malagasy Republic had been charming. The *Calypso* was placed in the hands of the workers in the naval shipyard, and for the next week they labored to remove the marks of almost four months of constant navigation and hard work.

The long evenings spent in conversation on the terrace of the hotel, dreaming of future projects and listening to the whispered sounds of the forest, far from the constant movement of the deck beneath our feet and the continuous murmuring of the ship and all its mechanical equipment, had revived our thirst for a new departure, new scenes of action. Beneath the apparent nostalgia we felt as we watched the land drop below the horizon, far behind us, we sensed the quiet enthusiasm which always accompanies a new beginning. During this week when we had been sailing north, we had imagined and prepared all sorts of traps we had never used before, and made our plans for new experiments, which would allow us, perhaps, to arrive at a better understanding of sharks.

But nothing had prepared us for this splendid meeting. The whale shark is certainly the largest fish in the world. He may reach a length of sixty-five feet, and a size of thirty or more feet is quite common. Encounters with this giant are rare, and no one knows precisely whether he follows a strange pat-

The whale shark is certainly the largest fish in the world. It is a shark, albeit totally harmless. This shark very seldom appears at the ocean's surface; it is fairly curious about divers and will not swim away at great speeds, of which it is capable. It usually swims leisurely in areas where vast quantities of plankton may be found. Although their shape is monstrous, the whale sharks are not likely to harm a diver with their mouth, but a stroke of their powerful tail would bear disastrous consequences.

tern of migration or is sedentary. He feeds on plankton and small fish, as do whales, and probably passes his life following the deep-sea currents which carry his nourishment from one ocean to another. My father, in all his long career as a navigator, has encountered this enormous animal only twice.

The whale shark is a squalus with five branchial clefts, bearing the scientific name *Rhineodon typus.** He is gray-brown on the back and sides, with round white or yellow spots spaced throughout the body and the tail, becoming smaller and more closely grouped on the head. Sinuous bands of color, yellow or white, and very narrow, mark his back with transverse stripings. The belly is white or yellow. The mouth is almost always open, forming a gap as much as six feet in width and from twelve to twenty inches in height. It is lined with a surface of rough platings, probably intended to crush any prey which might be a trifle too large.

In spite of his colossal size, the whale shark is considered harmless to man. He swims lazily, at a speed not exceeding three knots. He is often covered with a large number of remoras and surrounded by a myriad of pilot fish of all sizes, from the thickness of a man's thumb to that of a tennis racquet handle. We had all heard a great deal of talk about this giant of the seas, but no one on board had yet been close to one.

As was customary on board the *Calypso* in periods of normal navigation, two men were permanently assigned to lookout duty and charged with reporting any form of activity that might call for investigation. Whether it was the air spout of a whale or a simple piece of floating wood, nothing was too small or too insignificant for us. My father's insatiable curiosity about everything concerning the sea had communicated itself to the entire crew, and the smallest unidentified spot on the surface was sufficient to warrant a detour.

Jacques-Yves Cousteau's narrative

Sunday, May 7. 11:30 A.M. The *Calypso* was cruising at ten knots, between Mombasa and Djibouti. At this time of year, the Indian Ocean, where it borders the coast of Africa, is still calm. The famous southwest monsoon is already assembling its forces, but has not yet attacked. The surface of the water reflects disturbing tropical clouds, but there has been no indication of life to attract our attention since the day before. Not the smallest school of bonito, not a single flying fish, and no sign of the blowing of a whale.

*The name is sometimes given as *Rhincodon typus.*

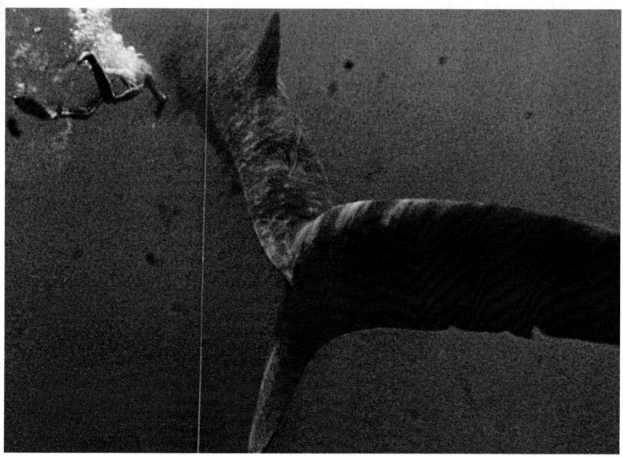

This is another view. The diver is swimming extremely fast to catch up with the whale shark, although the animal itself is moving very slowly.

The diver had been released from our launch some distance back. When the shark finally outdistanced him substantially, we picked the diver up and gained speed to catch up with the shark. After the shark outdistanced him again, the diver climbed back on board the *Zodiac* and we set out to catch up with the shark once more.

The sea resembles a desert, and yet the water is not very clear. The surface is laden with plankton large enough to be seen when we look out over the deck rails. This morning, we had spent a long time studying the passage of this stream of minute, erratic creatures, through the portholes of the observation chamber beneath the prow. They were simply white dots, or filaments, or little cups of crystal; a whole world of Copepoda, of jellyfish, of salpa. And all this population, of course, struggles for its own survival, obeying the same simple and cruel laws as the fish of the reefs and the beasts of the jungle. But their destiny depends on themselves to only a very small degree. They are carried about at the whim of the currents. They proliferate or die in mass, according to the caprice of temperature or salinity. This morning, the tropical sea was so thickened by the quantity of suspended living matter it contained that it resembled nothing so much as a gigantic bowl of hot soup, served for some unknown Gargantua. This ridiculous idea, which we had at first exchanged as a joke, was suddenly to find an unexpected confirmation.

At eleven thirty-five, Pierre Li on the port watch noticed something in the water and called it to the attention of the bridge. A few moments later Captain Roger Maritano ordered the helm to port, and the *Calypso* was on her way to track down the object. At first, we could make out only two large fins, separated from each other by a distance of many feet, but there could be no doubt that this was a very large animal. Soon, it became evident that it was not a species of marine mammal. It appeared, in fact, to be an enormous shark, half asleep on the surface. A pilgrim shark or a whale shark? We knew very little of either. The pilgrim shark is an impressive specimen, sometimes attaining a length of thirty feet. He makes an appearance in the Mediterranean during the spring (generally in April), traveling in little groups and swimming lazily on the surface. Then he disappears, and no one knows exactly where or how he lives during the rest of the year. But the whale shark is by far the largest and heaviest living fish of our time — if one bears in mind that the whale itself is not a fish, but a mammal. The whale shark is a pure shark, and only his size justifies his descriptive name. This giant likes warm and very deep waters, and comes to the surface very, very seldom. An encounter with him is a rare event indeed...

Excitement aboard the ship was intense. The *Zodiac* was put into the water within a few minutes, and the cameramen, Barsky and Deloire, and the divers, Falco and Coll, leaped into it. They made a noiseless approach to the somnolent animal, and the divers slipped into the water. The shark's tail was very tall and very long, the dorsal fin massive and rounded — it was actually a whale shark! He seemed interested by the *Zodiac,* and began to swim very slowly around it. He was about thirty-five feet long. Deloire swam closer, trying to film him with an undersea camera provided with a wide-angle lens. The enormous animal presented his profile first, and then came straight toward the camera. His open jaw resembled the forward end of a jet engine on an airliner. When he was no more than five feet away from Deloire, he suddenly submerged, just enough to pass beneath the diver. Coll, for his part, had equipped himself with his famous banderilla, with which he had already marked so many other sharks. He dived with the monster, and dived again; each time he was outdistanced he would climb back on board the *Zodiac.* When the little boat caught up with the shark, Coll dived once more. When he emerged from the water for the last time, he described what had happened, in his usual laconic terms:

"The caudal fin is six and a half feet, from end to end. The dorsal is a little over four feet at its base and almost four feet in height. The eyes are round, slightly slanted, and very alert. He sees very well. Twice, he came back for another look at the *Zodiac,* and each time that we approached him from in front, he lowered his head a little and passed beneath us. We saw him dive several times: he begins by inclining gently toward the bottom and goes deeper, in the manner of a submarine, but when he does this he comes back to the surface a few minutes later and just a little farther away. But when he had had enough of playing with us, he just swung over to a vertical axis and disappeared, straight down, like a sounding whale. I held on to his tail several times, and he did not react at all — either to attack or to defend himself. His skin is rough and covered with round spots, hard to see. There were remoras clinging to his skin almost everywhere, especially behind the branchial clefts. There is a cavity there, where they go in and come out. There was only one pilot fish with him, a striped one. I had trouble planting a plaque near his dorsal fin; the skin is very hard to pierce and I twisted the point of the spear."

A few minutes later, a second specimen of the same species appeared, an even larger one than the first. This one measured forty to fifty feet. Number Two, as we christened him, did not stay with us as long as his predecessor, but Coll succeeded in marking him and then, clinging to his dorsal fin, was dragged down with him as he plunged into the depths. Coll stayed with him to a depth of almost a hundred and fifty feet.

"At no time," he told me later, "did he even attempt to escape or to get rid of me. His only reaction occurred when we came into his line of vision, and the reaction was curiosity . . ."

Meeting with and filming the two whale sharks was a considerable stroke of luck. Why is it that they are so seldom observed? Undoubtedly because they come to the surface only under very particular and very rare circumstances — perhaps when, in especially fine weather, a certain admixture of plankton of which they happen to be fond is carried to the surface by the current. In fact, when we were able to study them underwater, our two prize specimens seemed to be swallowing enormous quantities of plankton in their gaping jaws. Baleen whales also feed exclusively on plankton and very small marine animals, and they are equipped to gorge themselves on this form of nourishment at a depth of up to eighty feet during the night and, sometimes, at a depth of as much as seventeen hundred feet during the day. The depth of the plankton varies with the light. The whales come to the surface only sufficiently often to breathe. Whale sharks, which are not subject to this need, come to the surface far more rarely, almost inadvertently.

Perhaps because of the similarity of their feeding habits, there exists another resemblance in the behavior patterns of whale sharks (cold-blooded fishes) and whales (warm-blooded mammals): we had just had an opportunity to observe with our own eyes the fact that whale sharks do not submerge by swimming toward the bottom on an oblique line. They *sound,* going straight down on a vertical line. No other shark does the same thing.

The divers had been particularly impressed by the enormous opening of the jaw, likening it, as I have mentioned, to the forward opening of a jet engine. The whale shark's teeth are very small, but they can be dangerous. Our American friend, Conrad Limbaugh, was once seriously hurt when his forearm was accidentally caught in this gigantic mouth. Although the shark, obviously, did not bite, Conrad nonetheless suffered extensive bruises and lost considerable portions of skin.

Philippe Cousteau's narrative

It seems natural that animals as fabulous as sharks should have inspired all sorts of legends and customs among the primitive peoples inhabiting the shores of the sea. What seems less natural is the fact that, in the majority of

such tales, the shark assumes the personality of a benefactor. He may be Kama-Hoa-Lii, the reincarnation of a well-loved ancestor, or the god of plenty, or even the protector of fishermen lost at sea. Never, in the course of all of my visits to out-of-the-way seafaring communities such as these, have I heard the shark spoken of as traditionally an evil animal. This attitude is all the more surprising when it is considered that relatively inoffensive animals such as whales are generally considered malefactors by most primitive populations. And other species, which are totally incapable of the slightest harm except in the event of an improbable accident, have a reputation as bad as it is completely unjustified. The manta rays, which are frequently called "devilfish," are a good example of this. In his book, *Sharks Are Fished at Night*, François Poli speaks of the superstitious fear in which the giant ray is held by fishermen along the coast of Cuba. Some of these men even claim to have been hypnotized by the manta, and there are stories to the effect that boats have been dragged down into the depths with their entire crew aboard, or that the monster has been seen to leap to a prodigious height and then fall back on a fishing boat, crushing it relentlessly beneath his fantastic weight.

All the books of discoveries and the tales of journeys across the seas in the Middle Ages speak of marine monsters enveloping ships in their tentacles and breaking them up like nutshells. Such imagery certainly contributed to giving the sailors of the time a reputation for bravery, which is well justified, in fact, when one thinks of the ships of that day and of their incredible fragility. It may very well have been a thirst for local renown that led these men of the sea to spread such stories. Although it is true that the giant squid actually does reach more than fifty feet in size, the appearance of such monstrous animals is extremely rare. During their crossing of the Humboldt Current, the members of the *Kon-Tiki* expedition saw many of them, several nights running, but fortunately they caused no damage. To my knowledge, the best example of an unjustified reputation for evil is that of the giant clam. According to legend, this warm-water bivalve mollusk is capable of closing on the arm or leg of a diver and holding him prisoner until he drowns or until the man himself amputates the imprisoned limb. Although this creature really does attain proportions of as much as two hundred and fifty pounds, the space between the edges of its shells, in an open position, is proportionately so small that it would require the abilities of a contortionist to slip even the wrist between them.

The shark, on the contrary, is an actual menace, and is present in practically all the waters of the world. However, perhaps in an attempt to reassure himself, man has made him into a beneficent deity in the majority of the regions in which he abounds.

Captain Young and several other writers tell that in the Hawaiian Islands, the shark was one of the most powerful of divinities. The shark king, Kama-Hoa-Lii, who ruled all other sharks, could assume human form whenever he wished. The legend states that he lived in a cavern large enough to shelter his enormous body, somewhere in the waters outside Honolulu. With the help of the powerful shark Kalahiki, he was thought to be the protector of fishermen in danger. He foresaw all the hazards of the sea, and therefore was prepared to come to the help of ships and crews threatened by tempests, contrary winds, or periods of calm. If they were threatened with such perils, the natives lighted a great fire on their ships and poured into the sea the juice of a plant called the awa. As soon as he received their appeal, Kama-Hoa-Lii dispatched one of his shark subjects — he never revealed himself — to act as a guide and lead the threatened boat back to its home port.

If the incantations were correctly formulated and the offerings pleasing to him, he could also become the protector of the oppressed and avenge the injustices of a tyrant or of a jealous husband.

The special ability of the shark gods to assume human form was, quite naturally, the basis for many fantastic stories. Some of these all-powerful beings made use of their unique power to seduce and marry the young virgins and beauties of the archipelago. Male children born of such a mating were all endowed with their father's powers, and the only sign of their divine status was a shark's jaw marked across the back, between the shoulder blades. The child's relatives were carefully instructed by the father never to allow the young god to taste of flesh, since he then would acquire a liking for it and cause horrible damage. It goes without saying that sometimes an overindulgent grandfather would break the law, and the child, in turn, would follow the villagers as they made their daily trips to the edge of the sea. There, he would leap into the water, reassume the form of a shark, and satisfy his insatiable appetite by devouring his comrades. If it was discovered that he had lost the cloak or "kapa" which covered the menacing jaw on his back, the young god must then throw himself into the sea and swim to a nearby island; there he might continue his murderous activities in a new hunting ground, where his identity was unknown.

In spite of such tales, the signal honor of being reincarnated as sharks in their next life was conferred on the wisest of all the wise men of the Hawaiian tribes. Those so honored were highly respected in their present existence, and a shark's jaw was tattooed on their back by the seer of the island. These gods-to-be were supplied with food by the villagers and lived away from the other settlements, in cabins built for them close to the sea, on the frontier of their future kingdom.

But it was not only in the legends of these islands that the shark was a very important personage. Archeology has revealed traces of ancient customs that were very real. Not far from Pearl Harbor, vestiges of marine arenas have been found, formed from blocks of stone set in the form of a circle and with a gateway left open to the sea. In this kind of theater, which is reminiscent of the Roman Empire, gladiatorial combats were held between sharks and men. Under the critical gaze of the kings and the people, naked men, armed only with short daggers, confronted deep-sea sharks. These weapons, specially designed for such occasions, consisted simply of a wooden handle bearing a shark's tooth as a point. It was, in fact, very ingenious since the skin of sharks is extremely tough and a razor-sharp tooth is one of the rare instruments capable of piercing it. Moreover, Hawaii at that time still knew nothing of the uses of hard metals. The archeologists cannot tell us how such combats usually turned out — whether it was the man or the animal who was most often the victor, or what sort of festivities crowned the games in honor of the all-powerful and generous Kama-Hoa-Lii, the great shark god.

But if the archeologists are incapable of satisfying our curiosity as to

This is a nurse shark, technically called *Genglymos-toma cirratum*. Nurse sharks, closely related to sand sharks, are extremely supple and swim almost like snakes. They seem to be nearsighted, and they hide in crevices for long periods of time. One method of getting them out of those crevices—tugging at their tail—has been employed, but it can prove quite harmful. It was a shark of this type that we encountered on Shab Arab, but that one was much bigger.

the outcome of these Hawaiian aquatic *corridas,* we can find an answer to the question at another point of the globe. The peoples of the West Indies, like those of the Pacific Islands, are in constant contact with the sea and have always had many excellent sailors and fishermen. Sharks are abundant and active in this region, too, and although they are not the object of such passionate cults, they are the subject of a great many tales. On the island of Santo Domingo, I have been told the story of two Negroes who regularly did battle with sharks. There was no special arena, but just a shallow lagoon linked to the sea by a canal which could be closed with stones and branches of trees. No dagger with a shark-tooth point was used, but a solid blade of the best steel. Once a large shark had been trapped in the lagoon and a predetermined sum of money paid over, the gladiator, armed only with this blade, entered the water, and a fight to the death began. More often than not, it went on for only a few seconds before the man succeeded in planting his weapon in the animal's side. Since these two men made their living from this dangerous sport, it would seem that they fought frequently and were generally the winners. Regardless of this, confronting a man-eating shark in the muddy waters of a lagoon demonstrates either a quality of courage that is extremely rare or a phenomenal inability to recognize danger.

In Central America, we again come across the belief that the shark is a beneficent animal, and more or less taboo. François Poli, in the book I have already mentioned, *Sharks Are Fished at Night,* tells of the almost ritual fear of the natives living along the shores of Lake Nicaragua, when they are asked to go fishing for sharks. These lake sharks are fresh-water sharks, remote descendants of sea sharks who have gradually become acclimatized to their new condition. There are some theories to the effect that when the mountain chain which shelters the lake was formed, a pocket of sea water was separated from the rest of the ocean. Over the course of centuries, this water became fresh water and the sharks it contained adapted themselves to it. This acclimatization is not surprising when one remembers certain species of South African sharks who pass a portion of their lives in the brackish waters at the mouths of rivers. Some have even mounted the Zambezi River to a distance of three hundred and forty miles from the coast, where the water, quite obviously, is perfectly fresh. The sharks of Lake Nicaragua have been definitely established as being related to these "Zambezi sharks."

François Poli also recounts how the Indians of this lake region, in accordance with ancient custom, would adorn the bodies of the dead with all their jewelry and then consign the body to the sharks. Hearing of this custom, a Dutch adventurer decided to put the primitive beliefs of the natives to his own use. He set himself up in a house situated near the spot where these burial-sacrifice ceremonies were held, and went shark hunting immediately after each one. It was said that he accumulated a considerable fortune before his activities were discovered by the Indians, but then he was murdered and his house burned to the ground.

The only occasion on which the Indians enter into conflict with the lake sharks occurs when, through misfortune, one of them is bitten by a shark and loses an arm or a leg. Then the hunt for the guilty animal is relentless, until the amputated limb is recovered and can be buried beside the victim, so that he may obtain entrance to paradise.

In the winter of 1967, my brother, Jean-Michel, preceded the *Calypso* into the port of Tuléar, on the southern coast of the Malagasy Republic, in order to make the necessary preparations for our stopover there. While waiting for us to arrive, he had many conversations with people living in the region and was told by a little girl that the members of her tribe had absolutely no fear of sharks, since they believed them to be the reincarnation of their ancestors. "And," the little girl said, "grandfather would not hurt me, would he?" These people are also among those who are convinced that in the event of a shipwreck, sharks will appear and guide their descendants safely back to shore. Obviously, no one in all this region hunts for sharks, with the exception of a few "vasa," white foreigners, who are considered sacrilegious.

On the sand beach of a tiny island in the Mozambique Channel, north-

west of Madagascar, there exists the only shark fishery of the entire island continent. Here, an old Arab who does not share the beliefs of the Malagasy natives stretches out lines from the edge of the shore and catches an appreciable number of sharks every night. As recently as a few years ago, he also gathered in the remoras — the extremely powerful sucking fish that attach themselves to sharks — and sold them, alive, to the tribes of fishermen in the other islands of the channel. The new owners of these fish attached them by the tail to a solid length of fishing cord and then set them free in the waters along the barrier of the reefs. Once liberated in this fashion, the remoras often attached themselves to others of the large fish or to the turtles in which these waters abound, and the hosts they had selected were then hauled in and sold. This delightful custom has now practically disappeared, and with it has gone a tidy source of income for the shark fisherman. Now, he tans the skins of his victims and presses their livers. These occupations, although considerably less romantic, provide him with a peaceful and happy existence, despite the foul odor of the tannery and the mistrust of his neighbors, who regard him as little less than a sorcerer.

In the marvelous islands of Polynesia, the attitude of the people toward sharks varies greatly, from one island, even from one tribe, to another. They certainly are not always considered gods, and sometimes they are simply ignored. In some tribes, the only precaution taken by parents and relatives is to capture a certain number of the monsters and close them up in vast, shallow lagoons where their children go to play every day. In this manner, the young people, who will depend on the sea for more than half their food, learn from their earliest days to understand and to control the sharks. Later in life, if they encounter sharks in the course of their fishing, they will know what attitude to assume and will not give in to panic. I know, from experience, that a shark confined in very shallow water moves with difficulty, and that the agility of Polynesian children is incredible to see; so the risk of accidents in these lagoons is reduced to a minimum. The wisdom of the idea is, therefore, quite striking, since this ancient custom eliminates the factor of panic and uncontrolled reactions which are so common in encounters of men with sharks. An American scientist, William Murphy, is intending to engage in extensive study of the psychological factors which intervene when a man is attacked by a shark, with the goal of augmenting the safety of swimmers and divers. He thinks — and, I believe, rightly so — that the unreasoning fear which takes hold of men confronted with sharks transforms swimmers from

worthy opponents into easy prey. His research, if it leads to a better understanding of the psychological relationship between men and sharks, could be
the basis for truly effective methods of defense.

In the Philippines, a combination of animism and a belief in the trans-
mutation of souls into the bodies of animals forms the basis of many local
religions; animals that could be used as much-needed food sources are, on
the contrary, tamed and abundantly fed. These practices transform wild animals ranging from birds to river eels into family pets. All are considered to
be the reincarnation of ancestors.

Happily, the taboo applies in a Filipino family to only one or two species.
Some families respect serpents, others hogs, and still others parrots, and a
family has no compunction whatever about killing and eating the sacred animals held in veneration by its neighbor. It is quite normal, therefore, to make
a feast of the reincarnation of ancestors — provided they are not your own.

I have already noted some of the roles accorded to the shark-god in the
Hawaiian Islands — at a time when they were still known as the Sandwich
Islands — but there is one that is perhaps most important. In all the villages,
each family selected a totem of its own, and one of the most respected was
that of the shark. If a stillborn child was born to a man who worshiped the
shark-god, he would attempt, by means of magic, to transfer the soul of the

This is the dusky shark dashing in front of the camera out in the open sea. Another beautiful sight in the underwater world.

unfortunate baby into the body of a shark. To perform such an operation successfully, the father wrapped offerings of fruits and sacred roots in a ritual matting of straw, and placed the body of the child with these. Then, after many prayers and incantations, he confided the precious package to the sea, hoping that it would be favorably received by the god. If the divinity accepted the sacrifice, he would, in turn, protect all the other members of the family against attacks from his servants.

In a temple dedicated to the shark-god in the mountains behind the sea, priests, whose skin was constantly bathed in rock salt and water, so that it eventually seemed to be covered with scales, predicted the exact moment at which the god accepted the offering and transformed the little body into a shark. The moment of this announcement was accompanied by rejoicing on the part of the family, and a banquet was offered in honor of the priests.

Many of the customs and beliefs of primitive peoples reflect their fear and impotence in the face of natural phenomena and dangerous animals. Almost everywhere in the world, volcanoes, earthquakes, tigers, or serpents are honored and feared — or rather, they are honored because they are feared. In most cases, however, these invincible forces were, or still are, represented by malignant deities. In the case of the shark, one of the most dangerous of all animals, this generality holds true only in very rare instances. The shark-god is always powerful and respected, but generally he is regarded as a beneficent and protecting deity. It is only in the minds of modern, civilized man that he has become an abominable monster, inspiring disgust and unreasoning fear.

Each of these two attitudes seems equally unjustified. If they lead to self-destruction, both adoration and fear are disastrous emotions, and this is particularly true with regard to a formidable animal. I cannot help but think of the wisdom of those peoples of Polynesia who teach their children neither blind worship nor irrational fear, but a complete understanding of the menace, so that they may avoid it and, if necessary, conquer it.

TWELVE:
The Study of Sharks
A school for sharks.
Open sea.

Philippe Cousteau's narrative continues

An experiment was conducted by Doctor Eugenie Clark at the marine laboratory of Cape Haze, in Florida, to determine to what extent sharks could be conditioned to respond to complex stimuli. Years later, aboard the *Calypso,* Doctor Clark carried out another phase of the experiment.

The animals used in the earlier experiment were of two different species. There were two lemon sharks *(Negaprion brevirostris),* one male and one female, three feet in length; and three nurse sharks of the same size, all three of these male. The two lemon sharks had been captured in May 1958, five months before the experiment, and were perfectly adapted to their captivity, in good health and normally active. The others, although naturally slower, were in similar condition. The theater for the experiment was an enclosure, in fairly shallow water, of vertically planted squared-off shafts of wood, spaced about six inches apart. The enclosure measured forty feet by seventy feet and, aside from the sharks, contained only a few large sea turtles.

Throughout the experiment, the sharks were fed five times a week, from Monday through Friday, and always at three-fifteen in the afternoon. Earlier experiments with all types of animals had shown the importance of regularity in feeding times. Therefore, for six weeks — the entire period of the experiment — a target made of a fifteen-inch square of laminated plywood was lowered into the tank at precisely the specified time. This target was lifted out again following each feeding period, and was never left in the water at other times. It was secured at one end of a wooden bar in such a fashion that it could be placed in exactly the desired position, just below the surface of the water, regardless of the height of the tide. To complete the arrangement for the experiment, an underwater bell was placed two inches behind the target square. Whenever the target was pushed back to this extent, the bell would ring, and continue to ring so long as the target was held back. As soon as the pressure against the white square ceased, elastic bands returned it to its original position.

In the first two days of the experiment — September 22 and 23, 1958 — portions of food were dropped into the water at points closer and closer to the target. As of the third day, the food was attached to the center of the target by a short, fragile line. In order to secure it, the sharks were thereby forced to press their snouts against the white square. During the first week, the sound of the bell was very feeble, but in the second week it became loud and clear, audible even on the surface. Each time the apparatus was lowered into the tank, a portion of fish was already in place, and as soon as it was taken it was replaced with another. This was done by sliding the food down a length of wire running from the surface to the center of the white square.

The duration of each feeding period was reduced from forty minutes to twenty during the second week, and continued at this length of time for the remainder of the six weeks of training — or, rather, of conditioning.

In order to judge the effectiveness of the system and test the results, the target was lowered without food at the beginning of the seventh week, and whenever one of the sharks pressed on it hard enough to ring the bell a portion of fish was dropped to a spot next to the white square. A period of ten seconds was then allowed the shark to take his reward. If he did not succeed in snatching it from the line within this lapse of time, it was withdrawn from the water. This was done in order to associate the memory of the sound of the bell with the presence of food. Each week following this, the food was dropped a little farther away from the target.

The results were as follows: although, at the beginning of the conditioning period, the sharks had shown fear when the target was lowered into the water, they rapidly became accustomed to it. In this six-weeks period, the lemon sharks took the food and rang the bell five hundred and twenty-two times, and rang the bell but missed the food one hundred and sixteen times. Thus, the lemon sharks rang the bell a total of six hundred and thirty-eight times. The nurse sharks obtained the food and rang the bell seventy-nine times, and missed the food ten times. As a result of their greater ability to swim in place, they were able to feed seventy-five times without pushing the target far enough back to cause the bell to ring.

At the end of the conditioning period, on November 3, 1958, the target was lowered into the water without food. Within less than thirty seconds, the male lemon shark swam toward the target with his mouth already open. When he approached the empty target, he slowed down, closed his jaws and brushed the target with his snout, but not sufficiently hard to ring the bell. After ten similar attempts, he finally pressed the plywood square with enough force to set off the bell, and a portion of fish was immediately dropped. At the end of the first week, the male and female lemon sharks were perfectly conditioned to ring the bell by pressing on the empty target, and then to return for their reward. The nurse sharks approached the white square very rapidly, after the food had been dropped, and after the second time they stole the male lemon shark's reward. During the first experimental period of forty minutes, the nurse sharks obtained three portions of fish in this manner, and even blows on the head from above did not disturb them.

Throughout the month of November and the first two weeks of December, the two lemon sharks came and pressed on the target every time it was lowered. Then the temperature of the water dropped below twenty degrees Centigrade and they ceased taking the food. This state of affairs continued for ten weeks.

In conclusion, it can be said that these observations had shown no disposition on the part of the nurse sharks to associate the target with the presence of food. The male lemon shark had shown a strong tendency to approach the target first; often, the female, although swimming in the immediate vicinity of the white square, would not attempt to touch it until the male had taken three or four pieces of fish. More than 90 per cent of the time, the sharks would turn away in a clockwise direction after striking the target. Since the food was lowered to the left of the target, the most rapid means of attaining it would have been to turn to the left, in a counterclockwise movement. The additional time required for a detour to the right often made it possible for the other sharks to steal the food. The male seemed to have a greater facility for effecting this unaccustomed turn.

On February 9, 1959, the temperature of the water rose to twenty-two degrees Centigrade, and on the eighteenth of February, the sharks once again began accepting food. The experiments were begun again on the nineteenth and twentieth, and the sharks immediately resumed their earlier habits. In two days, the male pressed the white square twelve times, and the female pressed it four. Then, after a short cold period during which they again stopped eating, the experiment was continued until the middle of summer. When Doctor Clark decided to disconnect the bell from the target, the sharks, after a short period of hesitation, continued pressing on the white square and received their usual reward. This could mean that the absence of the sound stimulus made no difference in their reactions, and it could have been useless.

The experiment did demonstrate that, under the conditions described above, animals of the lemon shark species can be conditioned to associate the pressure on a target with the obtaining of food. In a few rare instances, the first sound of the bell would immediately attract a lemon shark who was swimming at the other end of the tank. At other times, the male lemon shark, after having pressed on the target with insufficient force to ring the bell, would turn completely around and swim back straight toward it. This time, of course, he succeeded in ringing the bell, and would swim promptly to the spot where the food was being lowered.

The fact that the female waited until the male had eaten several times before advancing on the target herself suggests that there may be some means of communication between them which is still unknown to us.

The habit of certain sharks of brushing their heads against inanimate floating objects — and even animate ones, like people — when they are hunting for food, can perhaps be explained by a peculiar ability of the shark, as I have mentioned earlier, to taste objects simply through contact with them. This characteristic may be responsible for the relative ease with which the subjects came to associate the target with food during the weeks of conditioning.

One final remark seems hardly compatible with the legends surrounding these monsters of the sea. It seems that, at certain moments, they are quite playful among themselves. Once their appetite was satiated, they sometimes swam back and forth, pressing on the target but making no effort to obtain the food which was then dropped to them. On several occasions, the male pressed the target and then left the food to the female. To me, this was certainly the most *surprising* discovery of this whole experiment, and confers on the killer some slight aura of gentlemanly delicacy.

The following stage of Doctor Clark's experiments was to determine the shark's capacity to make visual discriminations between different targets. It was this experiment that we planned to conduct on board the *Calypso,* using sharks at liberty in the sea as our subjects.

Eugenie Clark was aboard the *Calypso* at Djibouti on Saturday, September 23, 1967, when we left port, heading north for the islands of the Suakin group off the coast of Sudan, where the sharks were already familiar to us.

The *Calypso* was anchored just in the middle of the canal between Dahl Ghab Reef and a small uncharted reef which we christened Calypso Reef. The discovery of this reef was entirely due to chance and might have been disastrous, since we almost went aground on it, but it turned out, in fact, to have been providential. It formed a natural barrier against the strong ground swell from the southeast, and created a zone of near-perfect calm in which we could drop anchor and utilize all forms of our small boats and the most delicate equipment. The experiment we were about to attempt was to be the last and certainly the most significant of the expedition. The circumstances for it were almost ideal. For the past several days, the atmospheric conditions had been

During a long dive in any water, even the warmest, loss of body heat is extreme. The sun is most welcome.

The red patches that you see in this bunch of squid are red tentacles. The tentacles turn red when the squid is in the process of mating.

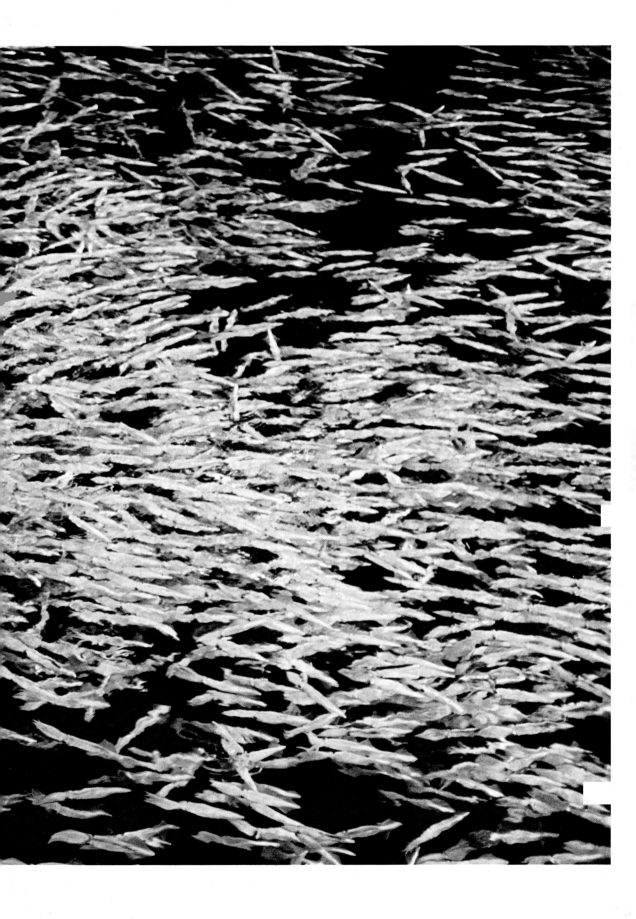

extremely favorable, and the absence of wind, the almost total calm, had allowed the water to clear to the extent that it was now of a crystalline transparency.

I have often noticed that the more clear the water is and the longer a period of calm goes on, the more active and glittering the life of the reef becomes. It is as if the movement of waves tended to carry the countless legions of timid little fish away from their sheltering clumps of coral. In order to survive, almost all the animal life of a reef has need of a hole, a crevice, a winding cleft, some branch or another in this immobile forest. Each of the little creatures, less swift and less well armed than any larger predator, depends for his very survival on the relative distance between the mouth of his pursuer and the entrance to his shelter of stone or coral. If the intruder moves toward him, the little fish draws closer to his hole, striving always to be certain of being able to reach it before the hunter can intercept him. If the sea is agitated, each wave creates a new and irregular current which obliges these little animals to remain constantly in the immediate proximity of their lairs, and the reef seems less populated, less brilliant, and less gay than it does in a period of calm. The fish, obviously, are perfectly conditioned to this state of affairs, and they know the near-futility of their efforts in bad weather, with the result that the constant hunt in which they must engage is really active along the slopes of the reefs only in times of flat calm. Since the action of the waves affects, to any major degree, only the first thirty or so feet below the surface, these observations are valid only for that region.

The experiment we were now set to attempt was scheduled to take place within that thirty-foot space, and, thanks to the persistent fair weather of the past days, the animal life here was proceeding at its normal rhythm. The predators had climbed from the intermediary depths, and were pursuing their constant search for food. Sharks, of course, were cruising among them, always ready to pounce on any wounded animal or to profit from any mistake in judgment on the part of a potential victim.

Doctor Clark had prepared the equipment to carry out here the experiment which had succeeded so well with captive sharks. This time, however, the sharks were free, perfectly at home in their element, and the behavior had not been affected either by capture, by unaccustomed imprisonment, or by an artificial period of fasting. We were all eager to go ahead, and the preparations had been painstaking in every detail.

Two square targets had been cut from panels of plastic, and painted with yellow and black stripes one inch in width. One of these targets was to be placed so that the stripes would be horizontal, while the other, although of the same pattern, would have vertical stripes. The two squares of rigid plastic were fixed in place at either end of a six-foot wooden bar. A small pulley was then placed at the center of the target with horizontal stripes and linked to a buoy on the surface with a pulley line of transparent nylon. This line, which was invisible in water, was for the purpose of bringing down bait in the form of pieces of fresh fish attached to a ring of galvanized wire. In this manner, we could send the portions of fish from the surface directly to the center of the target. The wooden bar to which the targets were fastened would be solidly attached to a fissure in the vertical wall of coral which formed the undersea façade of the reef. This façade, which is termed the "stay" of the reef, is a wall that begins at the edge of the coral reef and plunges straight down to a depth which often exceeds nine hundred feet. The waters surrounding it are the domain of the carnivorous animals of the deep, who feed on the leftovers from the sea-level plateau.

The sharks cruising in the immediate vicinity of the reef seemed to be sedentary, a fact that greatly increased our chances of success in the experiment. Working with the same subjects day after day should make it possible to condition them and to verify Doctor Clark's theory. A large steel shackle bolt and a short iron bar would furnish the sound source necessary for conditioning. Each time a shark seized the bait at the center of the horizontally striped target, a diver would strike the shackle with the iron bar, and the sound thus produced would be associated in the shark's mind with the idea of food.

This time, however, the experiment would be different from that carried out by Doctor Clark in Florida in that there were two targets, and we wanted to determine the shark's ability to differentiate between them. In the earlier experiment, the shark had only to learn to press on the target in order to obtain food, and the results had shown that some species succeeded in this without difficulty. Now, it would be necessary for the sharks to learn not only to press on the horizontally striped target to obtain food, but to select between the two targets, since, if they pressed the square with the vertical stripes, they received no reward.

In the first stage of the experiment, the horizontal square would carry portions of fresh fish at its center and the diver would ring his improvised bell. It was our hope that the shark would associate the design of the target and the sound of the bell with the idea of food. In the second stage, the hori-

The density of these animals is incredible. All those black dots seen grouped in two's are pairs of eyes. The bodies are almost transparent. They have no bones except what is called a feather, a transparent, flexible piece of hard matter serving as backbone.

zontal target carried no fish; the shark was to have learned to press on it, in order to have the diver ring the bell and then to be rewarded with a portion of fish. If he pressed on the wrong target (the one with vertical stripes), nothing happened. It was, therefore, a fairly complex experiment in two forms of conditioning that we were attempting.

Two days after our arrival on the reef, everything was in readiness and Canoë and I loaded the equipment into one of our small boats and set out to find a spot where the experiment might best be carried out. The requirements for this were fairly rigid: it must be an area in which we could not only attach the targets solidly to the cliff, but also find a shelter in a fissure in the immediate vicinity. We went into the water and began our explorations with a free dive, accompanied on the surface by the *Zodiac*, piloted by José Ruiz.

The spectacle we beheld was of a beauty as delicate as it was formidable. I swam along the edge of the plateau level, which seemed to mark the frontier between two worlds. To my left, there was a mysterious, disturbing void, which seemed to exhaust every nuance of color between blue and black. I could pick out vague forms, swift or lazy, lightly outlined in silver. They were tuna, powerful, enormous, and alone, ridged with scars of earlier battles. They were curious about us, and emerged from the infinite depths, approaching us, hesitating, and then swimming away. I do not know why, but even today this combination of power and silence impresses me. I am struck with a familiar and somewhat childlike idea: each of these magnificent fish has, through force of nature, lived for many years and engaged in incredible battles, swimming unceasingly through this world which permits me no more than awkward and too brief incursions. I was abruptly overcome by a whiff of jealousy — perhaps of love — and I turned away, suddenly conscious of being no more than an ungainly frog.

To my right, everything was reversed. The universe here was gay, vibrant with color and life. The sound of countless millions of tiny animals brought a constant echoing sound through the water, just as the strident sounds of insects carry through an Amazon jungle. It was a world of light and of serene mysteries, and yet, the combats which take place up here are no less bitter, no less pitiless than those that take place in the depths. In front of me, the edge of the plateau crowned the dizzying slope of a fringe of coral masses, extending out above the void like enormous petrified flowers. The swarm of timid little fish hovering around every jutting edge of stone shimmered before my eyes like a heat cloud on a summer day.

Canoë signaled to me, and I rejoined him immediately. He was swimming slowly around a kind of vertical fault which cut into the uniform surface of the cliff. On either side of the notch, which measured no more than six to nine feet in depth and six feet in width, the wall formed two advanced areas of stone, bordering the crevice as if they were two thick lips. The interior of the fault was riddled with twisting pathways and rich in hiding places, easily sufficient for a man. With a fluid, twisting movement of his body, Canoë dropped beneath the surface and swam straight down along the ledge, until he came to a little jutting branch of coral. There, he signaled to me that this spot would be perfect and returned lazily to the surface.

The region did seem made for our purposes and we set to work immediately. We fastened the targets solidly to the coral at a depth of about twenty-five feet. Just above and to the right of the targets, we prepared a hiding place for Canoë, who would be conducting the experiment. Since I was going to film the operation, there was no question of a fixed refuge for me; I would have to make do with improvised shelters anywhere in the area.

When everything was ready, Canoë speared a too-curious caranx and the sharks appeared at once. They had seemed to arrive from nowhere, and, as always, there was something of the miraculous about it. Suddenly, at a point very close to us, the water materialized into one and then two moving rocket forms, swift and disturbing. Their blue-gray color mingled so perfectly with the colors in the depths below that it provided at least some explanation for this apparent prodigy of nature. They had probably been there for a long time, watching our activity but outside our field of vision, and had not approached until they were alerted by the convulsive movement of the dying caranx. They were two sharks with white-tipped fins, *Albimarginatus,* audacious and fast. The larger of the two must have been almost ten feet in length, while the other was much smaller, no more than four feet long and considerably more nervous in his reactions. They seemed to have located the fish — which we had now planted at the center of the target — with no difficulty, but it was three hours later before they bit into it. Their age-old instinct constrained them to prudence. Our unexpected presence did not reassure them at all, and the way in which the food was presented to them was not the best proof of our good manners. The setting was unusual, and they disliked the colors. Through all this long period of waiting, neither Canoë nor I moved from our stations. The sharks would swim off into the distance and be lost to our sight, sometimes for quite a long time, but they came back and resumed their patrol in front of the target. Suddenly, a third shark, scarcely larger than the smaller of the first two, appeared on the scene, and that seemed to decide things for the largest. He made an abrupt full turn and swam directly toward the target. I started my camera, but it was a wasted effort. At about three feet from the target, he turned away again, seemed to hesitate for a moment, and then resumed his lazy swimming, back and forth, just in front of us. I think now that the scent of the other pieces of fish, which we had neglected to enclose in a waterproof sack, contributed to the sharks' confusion, and caused them to mistake the exact location of the bait we had set for them. However, I did not have to wait much longer. The largest shark, which, in addition to his size, was easily recognizable by a fin that had been cut almost in two in some long-past fight, turned back again, and this time he bit into the bait after only a fleeting hesitation. The sound of the improvised bell, which Canoë struck constantly while the shark was seizing and swallowing his prey, seemed to have no influence, either on him or on the others, who had closed in on the target as soon as he had seized the bait.

In the two hours that followed, the same shark took four portions of fish and missed his target four other times, while the smallest took only a single portion and the third shark none at all. We left the water after six hours of watchful waiting, exhausted but satisfied. The experiment was well under way.

The next morning, the same operation was begun again, but this time with less success. This session began, however, with a violent scene. When Canoë killed the fish we planned to use as bait, the big shark with the damaged fin surged from the depths like a torpedo, swimming straight toward Canoë, who retreated immediately to his prearranged shelter. Then, with a vicious contortion of his entire body, the enormous animal turned and swept toward me, his gaping jaws already opened. He was on a level with my head, and I could neither draw back any distance nor move to the right or the left. I tried to make myself as small as possible, and lashed out at him with the camera. I felt a shock and a sudden turbulence in the water that snatched the mask from my face, and then the camera was no longer in my hands. Flattened against the wall of coral, deprived of the mask that provided me with sight, I tried to make out the powerful form I knew to be somewhere just in front of me. I felt certain that he would return to the attack. It was only when the vague mass swimming in my direction was almost upon me that I recognized Canoë. He had picked up the camera, and it was he who

The vision of a large school of squid next to the ship at night is one of the more beautiful sights we encountered. Divers are swimming through them, and in the foreground is Delcoutère. Bernard Chauvellin is holding the lights next to Philippe Cousteau, who is at his left with the camera.

A quick surfacing to give instructions to Delcoutère and Chauvellin.

received the second attack. He managed, somehow, to evade it, and then found my face mask and held it out to me. I put it on and emptied it of water in a matter of seconds. The scene before me was clear now. The shark had gone back to his pose of nonchalant surveillance, just a few feet away. Canoë returned to his post behind the targets, and I checked my camera. Only the sun screen seemed to have been damaged, so we continued with the experiment.

This animal's attitude was strange, very unlike that of others of his kind. Never before had I seen a shark immediately attack, a second time, a prey he had missed completely on his first attempt. Moreover, in the course of the first attack, he had received a blow with the camera that was by no means negligible. Once again I thought of the phrase my father wrote in his book *The Silent World:* ". . . the closer we come to sharks, the less we know of them. No one can ever predict what a shark is going to do."

The experiment was continued for several days, and although its first results were extremely promising, we were forced to interrupt it. A cable from Paris announced the imminent arrival of a new doctor and two new members of the crew, and so we were forced to put back to sea, heading for the coast of Eritrea and the port of Massawa.

By the time we left, the sharks were coming regularly to the target with the horizontal stripes, in search of their meals. Throughout the entire experiment, I had never seen a shark brush against the vertical target. In comparing these results with those of Doctor Clark's earlier experiments, it would seem that sharks at liberty — the *Albimarginatus,* as least — learn more rapidly than their captive relatives.

THIRTEEN:
Conclusions
on Shark Behavior
Sharks among squid.
Understanding sharks.
Opinions for pessimists
and optimists.

Philippe Cousteau's narrative continues

We have surveyed the oceans but only to ridiculously slight depths, and all the inroads man has made have done little more than cross the magical frontier. Prisoners of air as we are, our ball and chain floats at the surface, allowing us only short, ephemeral escapes. Marseilles, Messina, Port Saïd, Massawa, the Maldives, Diego-Suarez, Dar-es-Salaam, Djibouti, the Cape of Good Hope, Guadelupe, Nassau, Panama, Callao, Cedros . . . So many angles to the path of our wanderings. Like ogres whose appetites are too vast, we have scarcely tasted of our discoveries. Too many visions have dazzled our eyes and flooded our hearts. There remains only a memory, trembling and deformed as a mirage, neutral as sleep. The irony of knowledge lies in its immateriality. Tomorrow I shall use everything I have learned, just as I do every day, instinctively, without being aware of it. But what have I learned of the shark?

The beauty of a supple line, the thought of possible menace, the exaltation of a combat in which I know nothing of the rules . . . but what more than that? I have learned nothing of myself: fear has no gauge, and action is but a need.

Yet, more than a year after my last meeting with a shark, a new adventure happened that showed me again the importance and the enduring effect of experience. At the end of March 1969, the *Calypso* was anchored off the west coast of Baja California in one hundred and fifty feet of calm and

Bernard Chauvellin is illuminating a shark right in front of him as seen through the surface.

The cameraman, Philippe Cousteau, swimming alongside the ship with masses of squid, which are illuminated by the lights held by Bernard Chauvellin.

limpid water. It was night, after a day that had been rich in action and movement; we had been filming sequences of gray whales, and sometimes we had leaped from our fast-moving boats onto their backs which were bleached by the spray. I was asleep now, deep in motionless sleep.

At about eleven o'clock, Bernard Chauvellin, our second lieutenant, who was on duty on the bridge, came to wake me. It seemed that millions of squid were surrounding the ship, forming an area around us that was white as snow. In the glare of lights from the ship, the whole surface of the water was a carpet of these animals, and their apparently disordered movements created a vast network of tiny waves, whispering through the air like the murmurings of leaves in the wind. Clinging to one another, multiplied to a number beyond reckoning by the reflections of their wake in the water, this multitude flowed back and forth like some gigantic hydra, flashing every color of the rainbow. The *Calypso* appeared to be surrounded by a living ice floe — but through the midst of it, swift-moving forms traced furrows as dark and irregular as the crevices of a mountain.

A dozen or more blue sharks of all sizes were striking lines of death through the living halo of the ship. Jaws wide open, the sharks swam slowly through the sea of squid, cramming their mouths full, then halted just long enough to swallow the gelatinous morsels in one great, convulsive movement of their bodies. Then they moved off again, still greedy, profiting from this incredible manna.

In its beauty, its darkness, and its vital cruelty, the scene had the aspect of a forbidden spectacle. We were intruders, allowed by some error to share a secret too mighty for us to comprehend. As we stood on the bridge of the *Calypso,* no one spoke. We could only watch this magnificent vision, in silence.

Sooner or later, however, we had to react. Within a few minutes, the cameras were ready and the underwater lights connected. The most experienced divers on board at the time were disabled with persistent colds, so it was decided that I would take with me Bernard Chauvellin and Jacques Delcoutère, who would carry floodlights to illuminate the scene I hoped to film. Bernard had been with us throughout the shark expedition, but he was not an experienced diver, and Jacques had joined us only recently. This was, in fact, his first mission. Bernard had taken part in several dives among the sharks of the Red Sea, but never at night, and although Jacques had been my friend for fifteen years, he had only just completed his period of training as a diver. In this living sea and this icy water, there is a great deal about sharks that would make an impression on divers far more experienced than my two comrades. But they put on their gear in silence, displaying no emotion. Then, as it always did, the dive began with the ungainly procession of the divers across the deck. We were, for the moment, awkward, waddling ducks, to whom the water would give some semblance of grace.

The shiver of water that closed in on me extended to the very tips of my limbs; the cold ran down between my rubber skin and my human skin, cutting off my breath for a moment. I was aware of the presence of Bernard, and then of Jacques, just behind me. Had I been right in allowing them to come with me to this meeting? For several seconds, as I watched the sharks swimming back and forth through the cloudy mass of squid, I was filled with apprehension. Then, quite suddenly, memory and instinct returned, and with them came certainty. The sharks would not attack — at least, they would not attack immediately. Just as it had been in our dives in the Red Sea a year before, I sensed, rather than understood, the ambiance of the water. The sharks surrounding us now were hunting and feeding on squid. They were concentrating all their faculties on a single situation. Only the taste, the form, the touch of a squid would bring them to bite. This was no longer a pack of wolves in search of prey. They had found their victims; it was an easy and abundant hunt, and they would not search for anything else.

We swam slowly into the zone of lights from the ship, and the reason for this enormous assemblage of squid became rapidly apparent. It was the mating season. The couples were swimming slowly together, one facing the other, their translucid bodies streaked with changing phosphorescence, their tentacles grasping each other in a multiple embrace. Sometimes, two or three other squid would attach themselves to one or another of the partners, like shipwrecked men clinging to a raft. A few solitary, more rapid individuals swam through the groups thus formed, sweeping brusquely from one corner to another, wrapping their arms around our face masks and our hands, around the camera and the lights.

The squid were gathered in such compact groups that it was almost impossible to see more than two feet ahead, and nose-to-nose encounters with a shark were frequent occurrences. At first, however, as I had thought, the sharks paid no attention to us. If, by accident, one of them bumped into one of us, he turned away immediately and started off in another direction, still devouring and swallowing the little creatures with which the sea was filled. We went down to a depth of about fifty feet, where the water became clear and dark again. Above us, the white mass of squid looked like a fleecy cloud. Bernard's floodlights attracted a few of the squid to us — either blinded or simply curious. Seen from below, the bellies of the blue sharks were astonishingly white, and their skin seemed very tender and fragile.

I had finished my reel of film, and decided to go back to the ship. But, during our ascent to the surface, I was abruptly conscious of a change in the ambiance around us. After more than an hour, the sharks seemed to have recognized our presence, and they were now reacting. The exploratory blows of their snouts were more violent, they were circling around us and coming back more often to brush against our diving suits, as if they thought they might perceive the true taste of our flesh through our covering of rubber. We were close to the surface now, and I could see Bernard Delemotte's face, as he leaned out of the boat, watching and waiting. A shark stormed brutally through a cloud of squid and smashed his head against the camera. He turned back, then apparently decided to attack again, changed his mind and disap-

The incredible number of these squid resembles a stream of white gelatinous matter going by the ship. They are usually very fast, but at this time of year they are very sluggish and consequently make for easy prey. This sight is fascinating as seen against the light on board the *Calypso*.

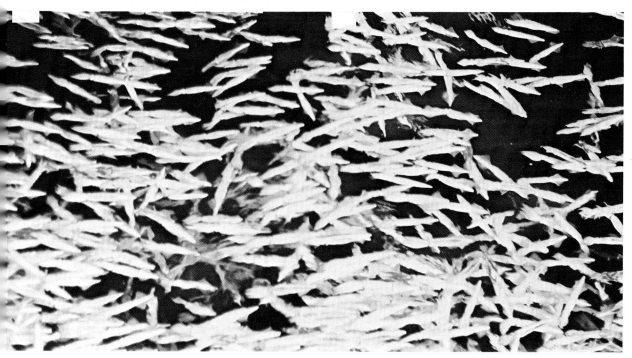

Even more discernible here than in the previous picture are the red tentacles of the squid.

peared. It was high time to leave the water. While Chauvellin and Delcoutère were ridding themselves of their equipment, Delemotte soberly told me that we had come out at exactly the moment when things were getting dangerous.

After all the months of forgetfulness, there still remained with us something of our adventures in the Red Sea: experience. For a few moments, I had the vague feeling of having acquired knowledge, and then the feeling disappeared. Many divers or swimmers, and many other people who simply want to learn, have asked us questions about sharks. Are they really dangerous? What species are the most dangerous? What can a man do against this animal? What are the best means of protection? And so on . . . For my part, I know that we have been protected in our encounters with sharks primarily by extreme prudence and great respect for the animal and his weapons of attack. Later, too, came experience and a more instinctive evaluation of danger whenever we made a dive.

Obviously, this kind of knowledge of the animal cannot be transmitted and is purely personal. A few simple bits of information may, however, help or at least prepare the diver for a confrontation with sharks, if it should prove inevitable.

Jacques-Yves Cousteau's comments

Until today, the majority of scientific experiments conducted with sharks have been carried out with animals in captivity. They are, therefore, interesting as indications of shark behavior, but they shed little light on the behavior of sharks at liberty.

Statistics concerning accidents due to sharks are still very poorly conceived. They center primarily on swimmers, and are almost always based on the highly disputable testimony of fishermen or on that of secondhand witnesses.

The observations of divers are more interesting, but they are infrequent and often contradictory. Moreover, the authors of these stories are quite often afflicted with a hero complex.

Experiments, statistics, and observations are all, therefore, subject to caution, and it is my considered opinion that it would be extremely premature to draw any conclusions about the dangers present in an encounter with sharks while diving.

But, if it is impossible to give this book very many *conclusions,* it is possible to express some *personal opinions.*

FOR PESSIMISTS

Every species of shark, even the most inoffensive, is anatomically a formidable source of potential danger. On paper, the most to be feared are the great white sharks *(Carcharodon carcharias),* with their enormous jaws and great, triangular teeth. But, in reality, this species is extremely rare. By far the most disturbing are the *Carcharhinus longimanus,* whose great rounded fins bear a large white circle at their extremities. These "lords of the long hands" are encountered only in the open sea, but everywhere in warm waters. They are the only species of shark that is never frightened by the approach of a diver, and they are the most dangerous of all sharks.

The youngest sharks — and therefore the smallest — are the most brazen. Even a very small shark, two feet in length, can inflict dangerous wounds.

Sharks race in from great distances to devour any fish in trouble. They can perceive the fish's convulsive movements by the rhythm of the pressure waves carried to them through the water. At a short distance, sharks are also extremely sensitive to odors, and particularly to the odor of blood. For both these reasons, underwater fisherman should not attach their catch to their belts.

Sharks are accustomed to attacking, without fear, anything that floats. They may, therefore, hurl themselves at the propellers of an outboard motor. This attitude makes them dangerous to swimmers, especially if the swimmer splashes about a great deal and makes considerable noise. For divers, the moments of entering and leaving the water are particularly dangerous.

The smallest bite of a shark is very serious, and may perhaps be fatal, since it always involves a considerable portion of flesh. In addition to this, the effect of shock is proportional to the quantity of damaged flesh. A victim of shark attack may die as a result of shock, even if the part of the body damaged by the animal's teeth is not vital.

There still exists no effective means of keeping sharks away from the area in which you are diving — either by chemical products, by sound waves, or by fields of electricity.

It is dangerous to dive at night or in troubled waters, and especially if there should be sharks in view, without using some strong protective device. such as a solid antishark cage.

It is dangerous to show fear of a shark; he knows this by instinct, and can profit from it.

It is dangerous to unleash the defensive reactions of a shark by attacking him (with a spear, a rifle, an explosive, or an electric shock) or even by frightening him (by pursuing him into a place from which there is no escape, for example).

When sharks are gathered together in a group, their behavior is unpredictable. A "frenzy" may suddenly take place, for reasons of which we still know nothing.

FOR OPTIMISTS

The real "man-eaters" are always "somewhere else." In Europe, the waters of Senegal, West Africa, are thought to be dangerous. But, in Dakar, you will be told to avoid the Red Sea and Djibouti. Djibouti prides itself on never having had a single accident, but people there will tell you that Mada-

This shark has just gulped too many squid. One still hangs from his mouth, about to be very neatly cut in two. The reflection of the shark on the surface is a beautiful, changing shape gliding through the reflection of all the squid. At right, two pairs of squid show different colors. They can change colors very quickly. The eyes of these animals sometimes glow as brightly as stars in a dark sky.

gascar is infested with sharks, thirsting for blood. And, on the island of Madagascar, if you are on the west coast, the sharks are dangerous on the east coast, and vice versa.

The species considered most dangerous are also, as if by chance, the most rare. But this isn't very logical. If the white shark were really so terrible, it is probable that he would be more widespread, and we would have encountered him more often. Those we have encountered (rarely) have fled from us, seemingly terrified at our approach.

Sharks never "attack" a diver below the surface immediately. For a time that may be more or less long, but is generally considerable, they will circle around you, go away, and then cautiously return. You will have time enough in which to decide, calmly, whether to remain or to return to the surface.

In clear water, and in daylight, a diver is in no immediate danger if he encounters a shark. A team of two divers can easily survey two sharks. But,

Sharks are tearing through this mass of food, eating as much as they can of the unexpected meal. The two sharks in the lower-left-hand corner are about to collide, unable to see each other through the mass of squid. They are too busy eating to notice the divers. They often bumped into us unknowingly.

no matter how large the number of divers, it is always prudent to organize some form of shelter if there are three or more sharks surrounding you.

A solid object, two to three feet long, such as a film camera or, better still, a shark billy, constitutes effective protection against one or two sharks. The extremity of the shark billy should be provided with short points or nails, so that it will not slip off the animal's skin. It will serve the purpose of repelling the shark, and at the same time of increasing the distance between the diver and the shark. But, in order to avoid any defensive reaction, the shark billy should never be used to strike or wound your antagonist.

It is indisputable that many swimmers and many shipwrecked people have been bitten or killed. But to my knowledge there has been no documentation proving that deep divers have been wounded by unprovoked attacks — the divers themselves may have been guilty of what might be termed a lack of proper behavior.

The best protection lies in ease of movement in diving, swimming slowly and softly, and avoiding any abrupt change of position. Turn around often, to look back at your legs, which are normally out of your field of vision. If a shark should swim toward you, do not try to run away. Face him calmly, with your shark billy extended toward him. He will turn and circle before coming back to you.

If you have been cleaning or skinning fish, wash your hands and body before entering the water.

Today, even shipwrecked people can find a form of security in shark-infested waters, because of shark screens such as those we tested in the Red Sea.

All things considered, diving in tropical waters is actually much less dangerous than riding a motorcycle.

Now that I have summarized the lessons we have learned during twenty years of extensive diving among sharks in most parts of the world, it may be time to express my personal feelings. Sharks belong to the undersea environment. They rank among the most perfect, the most beautiful creatures ever developed in nature. We expect to meet them around coral reefs or in the open ocean, even if it is with a twist of fear. Their absence means disappointment for the divers, while their appearance is disquieting. When their formidable silhouette glides along the populated coral cliffs, fish do not panic; they quietly clear the lord's path, and keep an eye on him. So do we.

Appendix A

A NOTE ON PHOTOGRAPHY
AND
PHOTOGRAPHIC EQUIPMENT

All our underwater photographic equipment was built by CEMA (Centre D'Etudes Marines Avancées) in Marseilles. The cameras were designed by Armand Davso (from concepts by Jacques-Yves Cousteau), who used components of various existing types and make of equipment. They are not really dry cameras in watertight casings. The watertight casing is actually the outside of the camera. The inside contains the mechanism only — the spools for the film, the gate and the sprocket movement, and the shutter movement.

These cameras were designed five years ago and are frequently updated and perfected. We now have 16-mm. cameras with lenses ranging from the superwide angles to 25-mm. to 35-mm. focal length. In 35 mm. we also have the superwide angle and wide angle; 9 mm. and 18 mm. are commonly used, and we also have a 35 mm. for extreme close-ups.

For the stills we have built a watertight case for the Nikon camera, using it mostly with the 21-mm. lens. Of course, all the correction ports are ground by one of our specialists to the specification of each lens.

The film used is mostly in 16-mm. Ektachrome 7255. We sometimes use the faster stock of 7242 or 7241, although they are much more difficult to employ because of their low tolerance for backlighting and wide differences in the amount of light. They are, in general, too contrasting. In 35 mm., of course, we use mostly the Eastman Color 5254 and 5251. For the stills we use Ektachrome X or Ektachrome High Speed in 125 ASA. We also use — but very seldom — Kodachrome 2 stock.

For our underwater lighting we use 1000-watt quartz lamps, with a color balance for 3200 K Degrees Kelvin. We also use the same type of quartz for lighting for still photography when we can, and when we cannot we use flash guns with Sylvania bulbs.

A cameraman shooting a shark. He must get as close as possible and out in the open water to do that, although he is protected by another diver immediately behind him (not seen here). This shot was taken on a day when the shark was not too aggressive.

The topside equipment is composed of several Arriflex 16, Arriflex 35, and Eclair cameras. Some are hand-held, very tiny Bell & Howell cameras, used in 35 mm. as well as 16 mm., for dangerous shots which might endanger the camera, as in the case of dropping into the water. In the event of accident it is not very important if the camera is damaged, so long as the cameraman is safe.

Sound recording is made with Perfectone equipment and very directional microphones. The sync is a quartz sync system that allows the camera and the recorder to be separated, and not attached by a cord. The use of wireless microphones also facilitates the use of this equipment; because then there is no cord from the subject to the camera or to the tape recorder, or from the tape recorder to the camera. They are three independent units.

Appendix B

DRAWINGS OF SHIPS, SHARKS, AND SEA-GOING EQUIPMENT

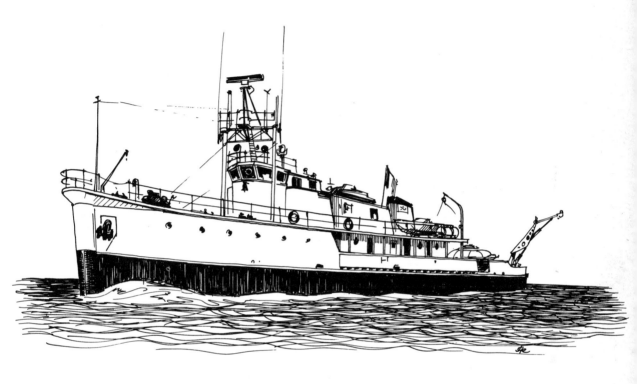

Figure 1. *Calypso*.

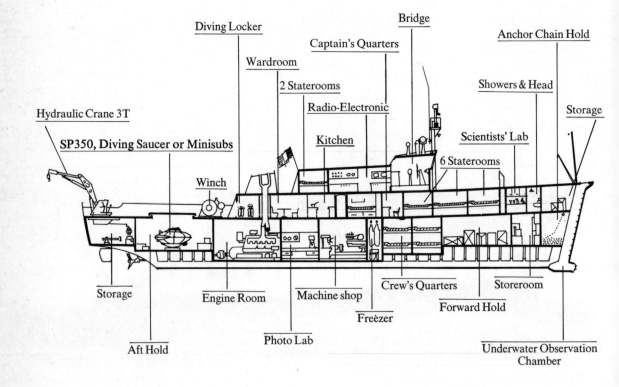

Figure 2. How the *Calypso* is organized from within. Illustrated are all the modifications made before her departure on this shark expedition. The roof and control room were entirely changed; bunks were added in the main deck, forward portion, and accommodations were made to give more space to moviemaking—to the cameramen and their equipment. In the aft hold, the diving saucer rests on a stand. Every instrument in this hold is devoted to maintenance of the saucer or the two one-man submarines, the Minisubs.

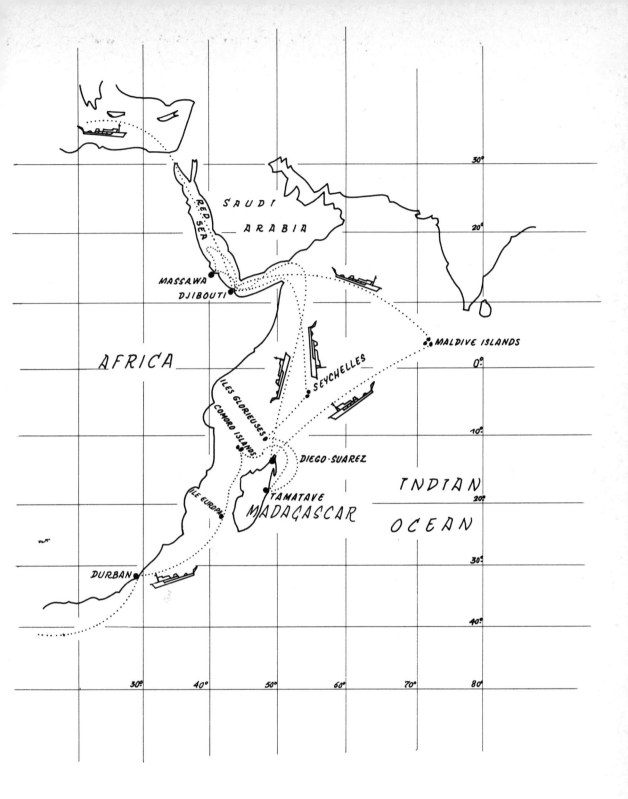

Figure 3. A general map of our shark expedition in the Red Sea and the Indian Ocean, indicating the areas most used by us. The *Calypso* left Marseilles in the Mediterranean in February 1967, went through the Red Sea and the Indian Ocean, and left Durban in the summer of 1968. The trip covered more than a year.

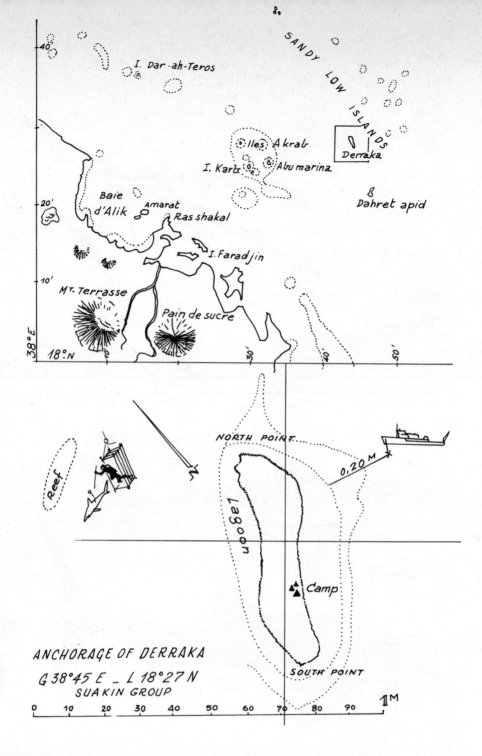

Figure 4. A map of the Suakin Reefs, which face the south coast of Sudan in the Red Sea. The lower drawing shows Derraka Island, where most of our experiments were carried out. The campsite is illustrated, in addition to the *Calypso's* favorite rough-weather anchorage. On the other side stands a small reef, which we dubbed "Calypso Reef" (it is uncharted) and the location where we did most of our tagging around Derraka. North Point was the most active area around the island, where we encountered the largest sharks and the greatest number of fish.

Figure 5. These are some of the most common species of shark. For comparative sizes see Figure 11. The dogfish is not considered dangerous, although it can tear some skin from a hand or foot. The mako shark is certainly one of the dangerous species, as well as the blue shark, the hammerhead, and the white-tip. Neither the thresher nor the whale shark is considered dangerous, although the thresher has a mouth that can inflict severe wounds.

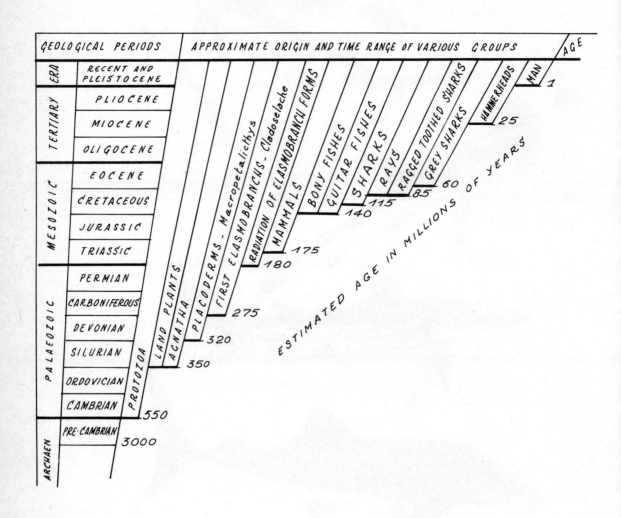

Figure 6. A self-explanatory comparison of the estimated age, in millions of years, of some marine species.

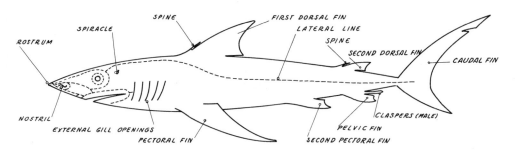

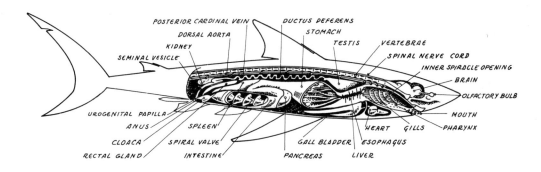

Figure 7. Both illustrations show the internal organization of the shark. Above, the location of the lateral line and most of the sensing devices grouped around the shark's head are delineated. Below are shown the shortness of the intestines, as well as the large stomach and extra-large liver. Inside the abdominal cavity the organs are not suspended by ligaments, and this is one of the shark's weakest spots.

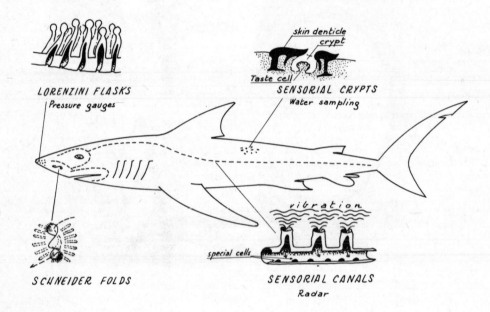

LORENZINI FLASKS
Pressure gauges

skin denticle
crypt
Taste cell
SENSORIAL CRYPTS
Water sampling

SCHNEIDER FOLDS

vibration
special cells
SENSORIAL CANALS
Radar

Figure 8. Drawing of the sensing devices of the shark. The sensorial canals moving along the lateral line are sensitive to vibrations and pressure waves. The Lorenzini flasks make it possible for the shark to sense differences in pressure. The Schneiderian folds cover the nostril of the shark, creating a canal through which the water flows. The shark's skin has sensorial crypts for water sampling and tasting of floating matter or possible prey. Most of these sensorial crypts are around the head. This combination of sensing devices is the key to the shark's perfect adaptation to his environment.

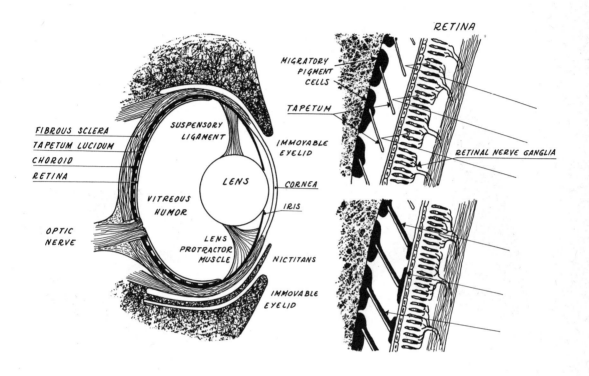

Figure 9. The interesting features of the shark's eye. On the left is illustrated the round lens of the eye. The shark's eye accommodates for distance; it does not focus by changing the shape of its lens, but by moving the lens in and out. In the upper-right-hand picture is shown how the tapetum, or silvery plates, reflect the light back through the retina, allowing the retina to be sensitized twice by the same ray of light. The migratory pigment cells at the base of these plates can be extended to cover the plates in bright light, as shown in the lower-right-hand picture, thus neutralizing the effect of the silvery plates. This whole system gives the shark's eye an extremely wide range of accommodation in both bright and very dim light.

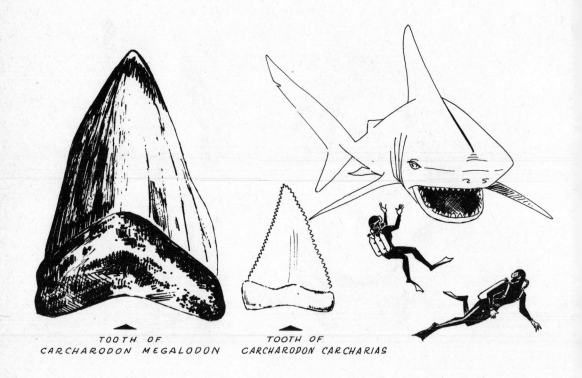

TOOTH OF
CARCHARODON MEGALODON

TOOTH OF
CARCHARODON CARCHARIAS

Figure 10. The fossil tooth of *Carcharodon megalodon*. This tooth is now in the Ocean-ographic Museum in Monaco. It was found in fossil layers. The shark to which this tooth belonged must have been of tremendous size, as noted in the drawing, which illustrates the scale of the shark as compared to man. The tooth next to it comes from a white shark (*Carcharodon carcharias*). The white shark is considered one of the most dangerous species and largest predators. The difference in scale shows what a monster the *megalodon* must have been. The wildest nightmare conceivable to a diver would be to encounter such a beast.

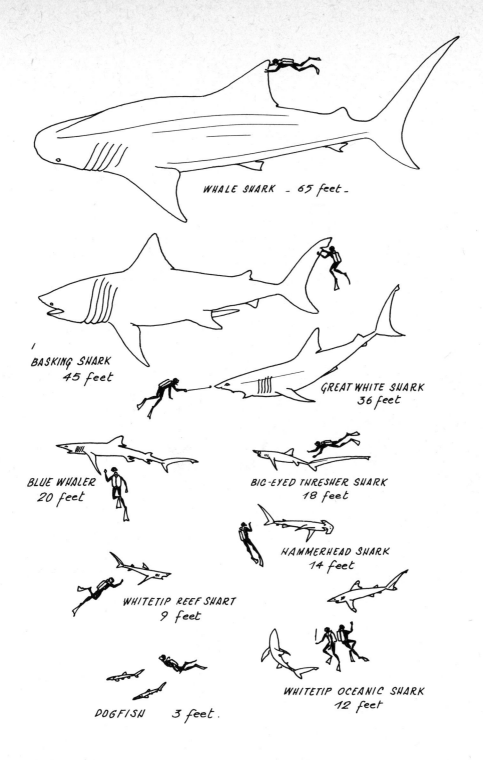

WHALE SHARK – 65 feet.

BASKING SHARK
45 feet

GREAT WHITE SHARK
36 feet

BLUE WHALER
20 feet

BIG-EYED THRESHER SHARK
18 feet

HAMMERHEAD SHARK
14 feet

WHITETIP REEF SHARK
9 feet

WHITETIP OCEANIC SHARK
12 feet

DOGFISH   3 feet.

Figure 11. A self-explanatory chart depicting maximum sizes of the various shark species, as compared to man.

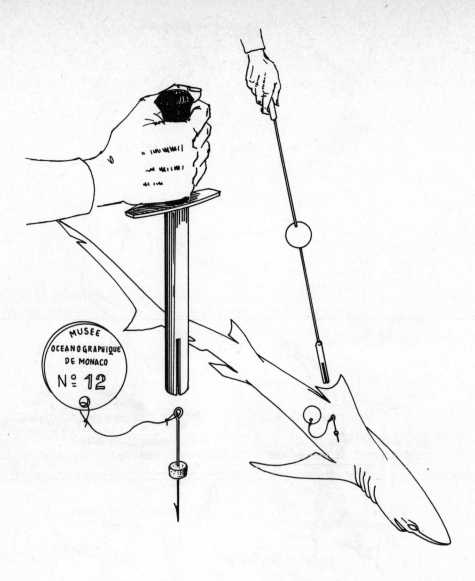

Figure 12. Our tagging apparatus. The short dagger was the one we used during the shark frenzies, because the longer one was not so practical. The long dagger was used out in the open sea, when there was only a maximum of one shark—perhaps two—not easily approachable. The tag illustrated is a sampling of what was marked on each of them. This is not a long-lasting tagging device, because the *banderillas* were made of steel, which would be rejected by the shark's skin after a period of four or five months.

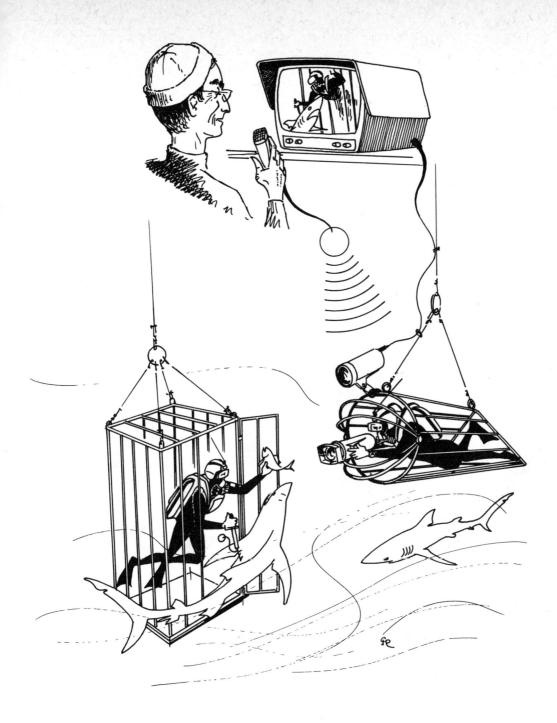

Figure 13. A shark cage used for the diver experimenting with sharks, and the cage used by the cameraman. This complete system is linked to the surface by television, where Jacques-Yves Cousteau, other members of the crew, and a scientist can monitor the action and communicate their ideas or directions to the cameraman, as well as to the diver in his cage. The system insures the accumulation of all data for the scientist on board—most of that time Doctor Eugenie Clark—and also makes for excellent safety insurance, since the viewer is able to detect danger and the cages can be pulled up immediately.

Figure 14. Depicted here is the equipment we used for filming the sharks feeding from the fish bait we'd caught, trolling in the Red Sea. Underneath the launch, *Calypso III,* are two movie cameras and one television camera. The cameraman aboard the launch sees what's happening on the TV screen and determines when to start the cameras rolling.

Figure 15. This is the setup devised by Doctor Eugenie Clark during her shark-behavior experiment in Florida. It is illustrated by a target with an electric bell, which rings in the water when the shark pushes the target. Immediately following, a reward of fresh fish is lowered to the shark.

Figure 16. This is the target experiment Doctor Eugenie Clark set up for us in the Red Sea, to help in our study of shark behavior. The diver just above the target is holding an iron shackle; he hits it to produce a noise, which contributes to the conditioning of the animals. The diver below him is holding a camera to record the experiment. The man at the surface drops pieces of fish, or whole small fish, on the vertical target, when cued by the diver.

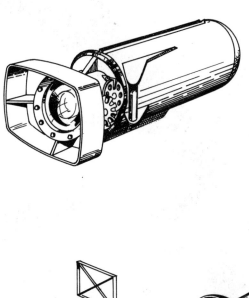

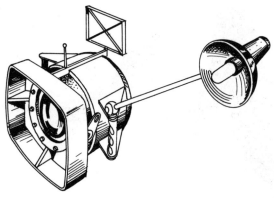

Figure 17. Shown at top, a typical camera used during our expedition. The controls are on the left near the handle, so they can be worked during shooting. On the other side is another handle, with a trigger to start the camera. All these cameras are made in our shop from Bell & Howell parts, and parts of other makes, and we use correction ports, ground to specifications, for each of our lenses. The drawing below illustrates a still-camera casing for a Nikon with 21-mm. lens and a correction port; also, of course, a flash gun.

Figure 18. A shark being attacked by porpoises. They hit the shark at top speed in the lower portion of the abdomen, the tender area of the shark, ripping apart the shark's delicate insides. They also destroy the gills by bumping them at top speed, thus destroying the shark's breathing apparatus.

Figure 19. Enemies of the shark.

The most dangerous enemy of the shark is man. Many hunt the shark not for self-defense against the killer, but merely for pleasure and excitement. Man seeks the shark to destroy him.

Boat propellers also tend to destroy sharks in the tropical seas. We have often observed the shark being mauled by the propeller of one of our launches or outboard motorboats.

The porcupine fish, which starts out as the shark's prey, becomes his killer when, as the shark begins to devour it, the porcupine fish inflates itself in the shark's mouth and asphyxiates him by preventing the water from flowing through his gills.

The great squid, too, is a killer of sharks in areas like the Humboldt Current. So are the alligators found at the entrance of Africa's rivers, for example, and the salt-water crocodiles, which massacre the sharks. The killer whale can devour a large shark at sea—an incident once witnessed by Professor Ted Walker near San Diego. Of course, as we have already mentioned, the dolphin is an eligible addition to the category of shark killer.

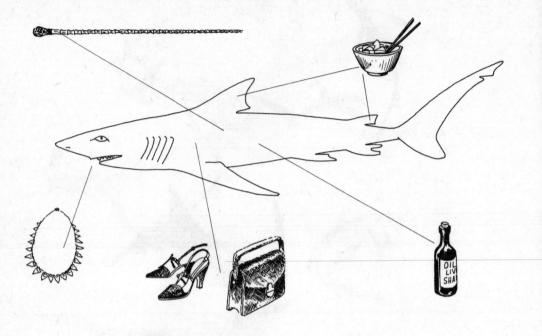

Figure 20. In many parts of the world, attempts have been made to exploit the shark for manufacturing by-products. Fisheries were once established—in South Africa and Florida, primarily. The principal product extracted from the shark was the oil in its liver. As shown in Figure 7, the shark's liver is extremely large and provides a great quantity of oil when treated. The oil, rich in vitamins, often was sold as cod-liver oil.

The shark's very tough and resistant skin has caused it to be used in the manufacturing of shoes, handbags, and other leather products.

The teeth provide assorted jewelry and ornaments, such as necklaces, bracelets, knife handles, sword handles.

The backbone is often used as a cane, supported by a piece of wrought iron which is run through the center of the vertebrae; the bone is filed and shaped. The handle of the cane is usually made of black coral, commonly found in the Red Sea.

The problem with the shark's skin is the treatment, which is a difficult, delicate process. The skin has a tendency to harden, unlike leather, which tends to be flexible. But this can prove advantageous, since the shoes, purses, and other items made of sharkskin are sufficiently resistant to last a long time. The skin has also been used in South Africa as sandpaper.

The fins are used by Orientals for food. In Lake Nicaragua, Central America, a fishery for fresh-water shark was officially established years ago. The fresh-water shark is a product of centuries of adaptation to these waters. It is related to the mako shark. The most important product of this fishery was oriental food for the Chinese colonies, made from shark fins. Today, most shark fisheries have disappeared. Cod-liver oil is usually synthetically manufactured, and shark leather has not proved commercially successful.

The shark is now fished mostly for its souvenir value in tourist industries of countries whose waters are abundant in sharks.

Figure 21. The squaloscope. Used for studying the shark in a confined area, the squalo-scope was designed in plastic and aluminum by Jean-Michel Cousteau. The structure proved efficient only for short-time study of the shark, because it was too small and the shark could not swim easily enough within the apparatus to ventilate its gills. After a while the shark would die as a result of lack of oxygen. The squaloscope was used pri-marily at Shab Arab Reef. It was not an easy structure to place in the water (being rather fragile), but it served an excellent purpose in allowing us to inject chemicals into the sharks to study their reactions. Most of these studies were made to determine the effect of tranquilizers.

Above the squaloscope, a one-man cage is being propelled, with the diver sticking his legs out at the rear end of the cage and paddling through the water. This mode of travel is absolutely safe, even in the worst shark frenzy.

Both cages were built in the south of France in our engineering plant, CEMA *(Centre d'Etudes Marines Avancées)*, headed by Captain Brenot.

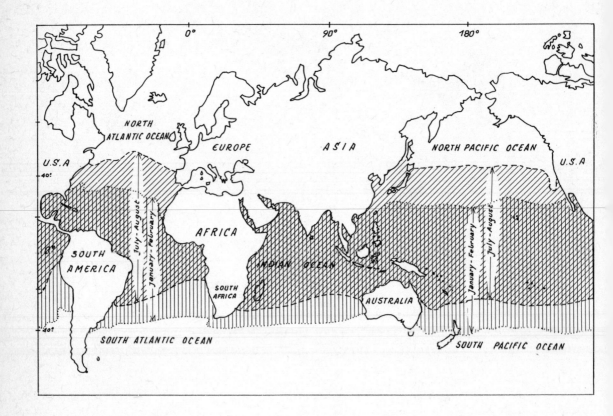

Figure 22. Illustrated in this map-temperature chart is the displacement, southward and then northward, of the warm-water belt around the world during winter and summer. This warm-water belt is certainly the area where most accidents occur. Most sharks are warm-water animals, except for the few species residing in the colder waters of the north. The warm-water belt is the area most often utilized by swimmers and divers, thus increasing the opportunity for accidental encounters. The chart was drawn from statistics accumulated by the Smithsonian Institution and other research organizations.

CREDITS

Photographers whose pictures appear in this book

Philippe Cousteau
Michel Deloire
Raymond Deloire
André Laban
Yves Omer
Ludwig Sillner

Some of the topside photographs were selected from the personal collections of crew members.

Drawings in Appendix B by Jean-Charles Roux

Drawings in Chapter 11 by Juliana Sloane

Researcher: Miriam Perry

Photographic Assistant: Joan Lavine

Index

Index

see also reef sharks
Wolper, David, 4-5
World War Two, shark attacks on sailors,
    113-16
World Without Sun, 172

Young, Captain, 173, 204

Zambezi sharks, 208
Zodiac, 4-5, ill. 50, 119
Zuéna, Paul, 16, 63, 66, 84-85, 95, 140,
    148, 152, ill. 11, 35